# Qigong for Arthritis

## - The Chinese Way of Healing and Prevention -
## Massage, Cavity Press, and Qigong Exercises

## Dr. Yang Jwing-Ming

## Disclaimer

The author(s) and publisher of this material are **NOT RESPONSIBLE** in any manner whatsoever for any injury which may occur through reading or following the instructions in this material.

The activities, physical or otherwise, described in this material may be too strenuous or dangerous for some people, and the reader should consult a physician before engaging in them.

© Yang's Martial Arts Association (YMAA), 1991

Second printing 1996
10, 2
ISBN: 0-940871-13-0
Library of Congress No: 90-71755

Publisher's Cataloging in Publication
*(Prepared by Quality Books, Inc.)*

Yang, Jwing-Ming, 1946-
Qigong for arthritis: the Chinese way of healing and prevention : massage, cavity press and Qigong excercises / Jwing Ming Yang. --

p. cm.
Includes bibliographical references and index.
ISBN 0-940871-13-0
1. Chi kung. 2. Chi kung-- Therapeutic uses. 3. Arthritis-- Exercise Therapy. I. Title.

RM727.C54                    610.951
                             QBI90-46

Printed in the USA

**YMAA Publication Center**　楊氏武藝協會

38 Hyde Park Avenue • Jamaica Plain, MA  02130
1-800-669-8892 • email: ymaa@aol.com
*Please see inside back cover for a complete listing of YMAA books and videotapes.*

**Dedicated to My Mother**
**Madame Yang Xie-Jin**

楊謝盡女士

# ACKNOWLEDGMENTS

Thanks to A. Reza Farman-Farmaian for the photography, Wen-Ching Wu for the drawings, Michael Wiederhold for the typesetting, and John R. Redmond for the drawing and the cover design. Thanks also to David Ripianzi, James O'Leary, Jr., Jeffrey Pratt, Jenifer Menefee and many other YMAA members for proofing the manuscript and for contributing many valuable suggestions and discussions. Special thanks to Alan Dougall for his editing; and deepest appreciation to Dr. Thomas G. Gutheil for his continued support.

# ABOUT THE AUTHOR

Dr. Yang was born in Taiwan, Republic of China, in 1946. He started his Gongfu/Wushu (or Kung Fu/Wushu) training at the age of fifteen under the Shaolin White Crane (Bai He) master Cheng Gin-Gsao. At sixteen Dr. Yang began the study of Yang Style Taijiquan (or Tai Chi Chuan) under Master Kao Tao.

Dr. Yang practiced Taiji with Master Kao for nearly three years. During this period, he learned the Yang style barehand form, Taiji breathing, and Qi circulation exercises. This was the beginning of Dr. Yang's involvement with Qigong (or Chi Kung). Through his Taiji practice, Dr. Yang gained an understanding of the fundamentals of Qigong training, especially the sitting practice for small circulation (Xiao Zhou Tian).

When Dr. Yang was eighteen, he entered Tamkang College in Taipei Hsien to study Physics. While there, he began the study of Shaolin Long Fist (Chang Quan) with Master Li Mao-Ching. At the same time, he advanced his Taiji training with Master Li. Later, he also practiced and studied together with his classmate Mr. Wilson Chen, who was learning Taijiquan with one of the most famous Taiji masters in Taipei, Master Zhang Xiang-San. Through these efforts, and through the continued study of Taiji and Qigong books, Dr. Yang and Mr. Chen were able to greatly increase their understanding of the internal arts.

In 1971 Dr. Yang completed his M.S. degree in Physics at the National Taiwan University, and then served in the Chinese Air Force. After being discharged, he returned to Tamkang College to teach Physics and resume study under Master Li Mao-Ching.

In 1974, Dr. Yang came to the United States to study Mechanical Engineering at Purdue University. Dr. Yang founded the Purdue University Chinese Kung Fu Research Club and also taught college credited courses in Taijiquan. In 1978 he was awarded a Ph.D. in Mechanical Engineering.

In 1980, Dr. Yang went to Houston and worked for Texas Instruments. While in Houston he founded Yang's Shaolin Kung Fu Academy, which was taken over by his student, Mr. Jeffery Bolt, after Dr.Yang moved to Boston in 1982. While continuing his engineering career, Dr. Yang also founded Yang's Martial Arts Academy (YMAA) on October 1, 1982 in Boston.

In January of 1984 he gave up his engineering career to devote more time to research, writing, and teaching in Boston. Dr. Yang has also travelled to France, Ireland, Italy, England, Poland, West Germany, and Switzerland to share his knowledge through lectures and seminars. Dr. Yang has written fourteen books and published six videotapes on Qigong and martial arts. The organization has continued to expand, and, as of July 1st 1989, YMAA has become just one of the divisions of Yang's Oriental Arts Association, Inc. (YOAA, Inc).

Dr. Yang Jwing-Ming

# FOREWORD

**Dr. Thomas G. Gutheil, M.D.**
**Associate Professor of Psychiatry**
**Harvard Medical School**

The book you are about to read further illuminates the application of ancient Chinese teachings and practices to contemporary health problems and extends the valuable contributions of Dr. Yang Jwing-Ming to the task of enabling Western readers to discover important long-unavailable Eastern texts.

The potentially beneficial expansion of the total repertoire of health information, by such addition of Oriental teachings on health and disease, has, regrettably, met with occasional ill-advised but powerful resistance. In September of 1990, Newsweek magazine carried a story under the heading "Medicine" which was entitled, "Does Doctor Know Best?". Newsweek told the following story.

A 39 year old Chinese woman named Julia Cheng, living in Connecticut, had a daughter named Shirley who had suffered since the age of 11 months from a severe and crippling childhood disease, Juvenile Rheumatoid Arthritis. As a woman from two cultures, Mrs. Cheng had had her daughter's illness treated in both America and mainland China. American specialists tended to use standard medications in the treatment of this crippling disease; physicians in China offered a combination of herbal and physical therapies. While the evidence from the child's own history seemed to indicate that a blend of Western and Chinese therapies brought some relief for the child's condition, her deterioration continued relentlessly, so that at the age of 7 (at the time the article was written), the child was in constant pain and confined to a wheelchair.

During the Chinese revolutionary period, the mother's trip could not take place, so that she had to seek help from a local physician. The child's Connecticut physician recommended surgical repair of the child's knees, hips and left ankle. The child's mother, by all evidence, presumably competent to make this decision, rejected this recommended operation and expressed her intentions to take the child to China (when that was safe) for less extensive surgery combined with traditional Chinese treatments (recall that Western-Eastern combined therapy had had some success before). However, the mother's refusal of the proposed operation triggered various child-protective actions by Connecticut's Department of Child and Youth Services, following guidelines in the laws designed to cover children thought to be at risk for parental neglect. Thus, the child was taken into custody by the public agency, and a superior court judge authorized the operation. For a physician in my field - forensic psychiatry and medical-legal topics in general - this case has many interesting features in several realms: the question of informed consent to medical treatment; the right of competent individuals to reject treatment (even, theoretically, life saving treatments); problems of cross-cultural issues in individuals who are making complex health-care decisions; racism and sexism in American medical and legal practice (as might relate to the fact that the patient was both a woman and Chinese); and many other clinical, legal and ethical questions. What I want to bring out here, however, and what leads me to begin my foreword to this book with this case, is that it reveals the perception, at least by our judicial system, and almost certainly of the American medical system, that Western and Oriental approaches in a real life case of arthritis were simply not reconcilable.

Note that Mrs. Cheng was not planning to give her child no treatment (i.e., to deprive the child of treatment); nor to give the child some idiosyncratic treatment (such as laetrile for cancer); nor to use non-medical religious methods of healing, as in some of the Christian Science legal cases that have been much in the news lately. Instead, Mrs. Cheng was planning to procure an active treatment regimen for her child, a regimen which drew upon a history of medical research, diagnosis and treatment extending back for literally thousands of years; and which, more importantly, had been empirically demonstrated to have some beneficial effects in this child specifically.

Understanding the regrettable case described above may have one indirect beneficial effect: it illuminates an inherent strength of the present volume. This volume makes as close a study as exists today of the application of ancient Chinese principles regarding Qi to the troubling condition of arthritis. Since many of the source texts for this study were only recently available, much less translated, this book makes it possible, for the first time, for Western readers to expand the repertoire of treatments for one of the most disabling of all diseases, by adding to any Western regimen this time-tested and systematic approach. Drawing heavily upon mental and emotional states, thought and mind, mood and morale, as well as upon what would now be described in Western terms as "low impact exercises," this text provides, to Western readers and sufferers of arthritis alike, an innovative and immensely valuable complement to the therapeutic armamentarium.

We must applaud Dr. Yang's efforts to make not only available, but also accessible and comprehensible, these ancient principles. While this volume fits best into the sequence of explorations listed elsewhere in this book, it is designed to stand on its own and to provide summary reviews of the basic ideas which it attempts to synthesize. The interested reader is in for a remarkably clear and organized discussion of a neglected subject area whose sufferers are legion.

# FOREWORD BY THE AUTHOR

## Dr. Yang Jwing-Ming, Ph.D.

In the last twenty years, the Chinese concept of "Qi" (or Chi) has gradually come to be understood by the Western public and accepted by Western medicine. It is now believed that Qi is the "bioelectricity" which circulates in the human body. Only in the last twenty years has Western science started to seriously study bioelectricity. Because of interest in this new field of study, and also because of more open communications with China, this field will probably bloom during the next twenty years. The most obvious indications of this trend are the widespread acceptance of acupuncture treatment for illnesses and the popularity of Qigong exercises and Taijiquan (or Tai Chi Chuan)(an internal martial art).

Practicing Qigong (pronounced "Chee Gong," the science of working with Qi, the energy within the body) can not only maintain your health and mental balance, but can also cure a number of illnesses without the use of any drugs. Instead, Qigong uses still and moving meditation to increase and regulate the Qi circulation.

When you practice regularly, your mind will gradually become calm and peaceful, and your whole being will start to feel more balanced. However, the most important result of regular practice of Qigong is your discovery of the inner world of your body's energy. Through sensing and feeling, and examining your inner experiences, you will start to understand yourself not only physically but also mentally. This science of internal sensing, which the Chinese have been studying for several thousand years, is usually totally ignored by the Western world. However, in today's busy and confusing society, this training is especially important. With the mental peace and calmness that Qigong can give you, you will be better able to relax and enjoy your daily work, and perhaps, to even find real happiness.

I believe that it is very important for the Western world to immediately learn, study, research, and develop this scientific internal art on a wide scale. I sincerely believe that it can be very effective in helping people, especially young people, to cope with the confusing and frightening challenges of life. The widespread practice of Qigong would reduce the mental pressure in our society, help those who are unbalanced, and perhaps even lower the crime rate. Qigong balances the internal energy and can heal many illnesses. Older people especially will find that it will maintain their health and even slow down the aging process. In addition, Qigong will help older people to conquer depression, worry, to find peace, calmness, and real happiness. I am confident that people in the Western world will realize, as have millions of Chinese, that practicing Qigong will give them a new outlook on life, and that it will emerge as the key to solving many of today's problems.

For these reasons, I have been actively studying, researching, and publishing what I have learned. However, after a few years of effort, I feel that what I have accomplished is too slow and shallow. The reason for this is simply that YMAA is young and lacks the financial foundation to handle such a large and important job. I and the few people like me who are struggling to spread the word about Qigong cannot do it well enough by ourselves. We need to involve more people, but we especially need universities and established medical organizations to involve themselves in the research.

Since I came to United States in 1974, I have dreamed of introducing the traditional Chinese Qigong treasures to Western society. It is only in the last few years that this dream has begun gradually to be realized. In 1982 YMAA was organized, and in 1989 YOAA Inc. was established as the corporate name with all divisions i.e. YMAA falling under its umbrella. YMAA has published two series of Qigong books. The first series is aimed at the Qigong beginner; the second series are in-depth books for the more experienced Qigong practitioner.

The first book and videotape in the introductory series are both called "The Eight Pieces of Brocade." The second book and videotape are both called "The Essence of Tai Chi Chi Kung." This book, "Qigong for Arthritis," is the third volume of the introductory series. It discusses the theory of Qigong and provides general information about arthritis.

If your curiosity about Qigong has not been satisfied after you have read through this book, you are invited to investigate the in-depth Qigong series. That series includes the following:

1. THE ROOT OF CHINESE CHI KUNG - The Secrets of Chi Kung Training (1989)
2. MUSCLE/TENDON CHANGING AND MARROW/BRAIN WASHING CHI KUNG - The Secret of Youth (1989) (Yi Gin Ching and Shii Soei Ching)
3. QIGONG MASSAGE - Qigong Tui Na and Cavity Press for Healing (Qigong An Mo and Qigong Dian Xue)(In preparation)
4. QIGONG AND HEALTH - For Healing and Maintaining Health (In preparation)
5. QIGONG AND MARTIAL ARTS - The Key to Advanced Martial Arts Skill (Shaolin, Wudang, E Mei, and others)(In preparation)

**6.** BUDDHIST QIGONG - Chan, The Root of Zen (In preparation)
**7.** TAOIST QIGONG (Dan Ding Dao Gung)(In preparation)
**8.** TIBETAN QIGONG (Mi Zong Shen Gong (In preparation)

The first volume, "The Root of Chinese Chi Kung" introduces the historical background and the different categories of Qigong, Qigong theory and principles, and the keys to Qigong training. This volume provides a map of the world of Qigong. It is recommended that this book be read before any of the others. The second volume, "Muscle/Tendon Changing and Marrow/Brain Washing Chi Kung," introduces the general concepts of these two arts, and discusses both their theory and their training principles.

To conclude, I would like to point out one thing to those of you who are sincerely interested in studying and researching this "new" science. If you start now, future generations will view you as a pioneer of the scientific investigations of Qigong. In addition to improving your own health, you will share the credit for raising our understanding of life as well as increasing the store of happiness in this world.

# PREFACE

Arthritis has afflicted mankind for as far back as we can trace. In all races, the young as well as the old have experienced the pain of arthritis. The condition can also have a disastrous effect on the sufferer's peace of mind. Despite the great advances made in many fields of science, Western medicine today is still unable to cure many forms of arthritis. Most treatment is limited to relieving pain and inflammation, rather than curing the condition at its root.

In the nearly four thousand years that Chinese medicine has been developing, many approaches have emerged to stopping the pain or even curing arthritis, such as acupuncture, massage, Qigong (pronounced "Chee Gong") exercises, and herbal treatment. Naturally, some methods are more effective than others, depending on the condition of the specific individual. Qigong exercises have come to be considered as an excellent method not only of preventing arthritis, but also of curing many forms of arthritis and in rebuilding the strength of the joints. Once the joint completely recovers its strength, it is well on its way to a complete healing.

In all of human history, now is the first opportunity that all of the world's cultures have had to get to know each other; we would be foolish to pass up this opportunity to learn from each other. It is clear that both Western and oriental medicines have their advantages and disadvantages. For example, Western medicine has traditionally ignored the existence of the energy (Qi or bioelectricity) part of the body and has paid more attention to the body's physical problems. Chinese medicine, on the other hand, has traditionally paid more attention to the empirical development of treatments and has ignored scientific research aimed at developing the theoretical background and more advanced equipment for both diagnosis and treatment.

If both cultures can share what they have discovered and learn to experience each other with open minds, then medicine would have a chance to begin a new era. Western medicine, for example, would be able to borrow the information which Chinese medicine has accumulated about Qi (bioelectricity) and combine it with the findings drawn from its own experience. Chinese medicine, on the other hand, could adapt modern Western medical technology to aid and improve the effectiveness of traditional Oriental medicine.

Arthritis serves as an excellent demonstration of how this combination of Eastern and Western medicine can work. Chinese doctors believe that the main causes of arthritis are weakness and injury of the joints. In order to rebuild the strength of the joints and repair the injury, Qi must be led to these joints and must be able to circulate smoothly there. Only by nourishing these joints with Qi can the damage be repaired . Chinese doctors have researched ways of improving the Qi circulation in the joints, and have found that the majority of arthritis patients can be healed. In addition, they have found that, once the joints are strong again, the arthritis will not readily return.

Chinese Qigong (energy work) improves the Qi circulation through both mental and physical training. In this book I will focus only on the Qigong practices commonly used by the Chinese to treat arthritis. Other methods, such as acupuncture and herbal treatments, will have to be introduced elsewhere by qualified Chinese physicians. I hope that this book will help many Western arthritis sufferers to regain their health.

The first chapter in this book will briefly discuss the general concepts of Chinese Qigong; the second chapter will summarize some information about arthritis. The third chapter will explain the theory of how Qigong cures arthritis; and finally, the fourth chapter will present some Qigong exercises for arthritis.

In order to be consistent with international usage, we have decided that in this book we will begin to use the Pinyin system for spelling of Chinese words. We hope that this will be more convenient for those readers who consult other Chinese books. However, in order to avoid confusion, commonly accepted spellings of names will not be changed, such as Tamkang College and Taipei. In addition, the spelling which individuals have chosen for their names will not be changed either, such as my name, Yang Jwing-Ming, or Wen-Ching Wu, etc.

# CONTENTS

# Chapter 1
# What is Chinese Qigong?

## 1-1. Introduction

Young and old, rich and poor, all have experienced the pain of arthritis. Because it is so prevalent, almost all cultures have developed ways of alleviating the pain or even curing the condition.

Generally speaking, younger people get arthritis less frequently than the elderly because their bodies are in better condition, and they are more active. Experience has also shown that, once younger people do develop arthritis, they recover more easily. Poor people have tended to get arthritis less frequently than wealthier people, because they engage in more manual labor. This seems to indicate that people who exercise regularly have a better chance of staying healthy and free from arthritis.

Like other cultures, the Chinese also suffer both physically and mentally from arthritis. Many methods of healing and prevention have been developed within the tradition of Chinese medicine.

The most fundamental principle of Chinese medicine is the concept of Qi (pronounced "Chee," known today in the West as bioelectricity). Illnesses are diagnosed by evaluating the condition of the body's Qi and interpreting the visible physical symptoms. According to Chinese medicine, when the need for Qi and its supply start to become unbalanced, the physical body is affected and begins to be damaged. This can happen both if the body is too Yin (deficient in Qi) or too Yang (with an excess of Qi). When Chinese physicians diagnose any disease or condition, they explore how and where the Qi is unbalanced. Once the Qi imbalance is corrected and the Qi returned to its normal level, the root cause of the illness has been removed.

Acupuncture is a common method for adjusting the Qi and preventing further physical damage. The Qi level can also be raised or lowered to stimulate the repair of the damage.

Applying Qi theory to arthritis can clear up many mysteries which cannot be explained by Western medicine. For example, almost all Western studies have denied that arthritis is significantly affected by the weather, despite the insistence of many arthritis sufferers. However, if we accept the fact that our bodies have a bioelectric field, it should be obvious that it would be affected by a strong natural electric field such as that found in thunderclouds. In fact, this external natural electric field can also disturb our emotions, since they are also affected by Qi imbalances in our body. Recently, the West has discovered that our internal bioelectric field can be disturbed by the electromagnetic field generated by high tension wires, and that this may cause cancer.

In China, acupuncture is not the only method used to correct the Qi imbalance that causes arthritis. Massage, cavity press (acupressure), and certain Qigong (pronounced "Chee Gong") exercises are also used. Most of these methods were created by medical doctors, but some were also created by masters of the Qigong systems used by martial artists. This is not as odd as it would at first seem. Since joint injuries are common among martial artists, many of these injuries would have developed into arthritis, a dangerous condition in a time when martial arts were used in deadly earnest. Many of the masters were experienced in Qigong and in elements of medicine, especially in the treatment of injuries, much like our modern "sports medicine" specialists. It would therefore be natural for them to find ways to treat a common condition like arthritis. Most people in the West are familiar with the slow, relaxed movements of Taijiquan (or Tai Chi Chuan). In China, this art is well known for its ability to rebuild the strength of the joints and cure the causes of arthritis.

While Western medicine has developed according to the principle of diagnosing visible symptoms and curing visible physical damage, Chinese medicine may be more advanced in that it deals with the body's Qi. On the other hand, Chinese medicine is still far behind Western medicine in the study of and research on the physical aspect of the human body. This can be seen in Western scientific methods and in the technology the West has developed. Because of the differences between the two systems of medicine, there are still large gaps in mankind's understanding of the body. I believe that if both medical cultures can learn and borrow from each other, these remaining gaps can soon be filled, and medicine as a whole will be able to take a giant step forward.

The ease of communication and the increased friendship among many different cultures during the last two decades has given mankind an unprecedented opportunity to share such things as medical concepts. We should all take advantage of this and open our minds to the knowledge and experiences of other peoples. I sincerely hope that this takes place, especially in the field of medicine. This goal has been my motivation in writing this book. Because of my limited knowledge, I can only offer this little volume. I hope that it generates widening ripples of interest in sharing and exchanging with other cultures.

## 1-2. The Definition of Qi and Qigong

**What is Qi?**

In order to understand Qigong, you must first understand what Qi is. Qi is the energy or natural force which fills the universe. There are three general types of Qi. Heaven (the sky or universe) has Heaven Qi (Tian Qi), which is made up of the forces which the heavenly bodies exert on the earth, such as sunshine, moonlight, and the moon's effect on the tides (its gravity). The Earth has Earth Qi (Di Qi), which absorbs the Heaven Qi, and is influenced by it. Man has Human Qi (Ren Qi), which is influenced by the other two. In ancient times, the Chinese believed that it was Heaven Qi which controlled the weather, climate, and natural disasters. When this Qi or energy field loses its balance, it strives to rebalance itself. Then the wind must blow, rain must fall, even tornados and hurricanes must happen in order for the Heaven Qi to reach a new energy balance. Heaven Qi also affects Human Qi, and divination and astrology are attempts to explain this.

Under Heaven Qi is the Earth Qi. It is influenced and controlled by the Heaven Qi. For example, too much rain will force a river to flood or change its path. Without rain, the plants will die. The Chinese believe that Earth Qi is made up of lines and patterns of energy, as well as the earth's magnetic field and the heat concealed underground. These energies must also balance, otherwise disasters such as earthquakes will occur. When the Qi of the earth is balanced, plants will grow and animals will prosper. Also, each individual person, animal, and plant has its own Qi field, which always seeks to be balanced. When any individual thing loses its balance, it will sicken, die, and decompose. Thus, the prevailing themes are balance, harmony, and interactive influence.

You must understand that all natural things, including man, grow within, and are influenced by, the natural cycles of Heaven Qi and Earth Qi. Since you are part of this nature (Dao or Tao), you must understand Heaven Qi and Earth Qi. Only then will you be able to adjust yourself, when necessary, to fit more smoothly into the natural cycle, and you will learn how to protect yourself from the negative influences in nature. This condition is the major goal of Qigong practice.

The Chinese have researched nature for thousands of years. Some of the information on the patterns and cycles of nature has been recorded in books, one of which is the Yi Jing (or I Ching)(Classic of Changes). Like an almanac, this book gives the average person formulas to trace when the seasons will change, when it will snow, even when a farmer should plow or harvest. You must remember that nature is always repeating itself. If you observe carefully, you will be able to see many of these routine patterns and cycles caused by the rebalancing of the Qi fields.

Over thousands of years the Chinese have researched the interrelationships of all things in nature, especially in regard to human beings. From this experience they have created various Qigong exercises to help bring the body's Qi circulation into harmony with nature's cycles. This helps to avoid illnesses caused by weather or seasonal changes.

After a long period of research and study, the Chinese also discovered that through Qigong practice they were able to strengthen their Qi and slow down the degeneration of the body, gaining not only health but also a longer life. The realization that such results were possible greatly spurred new research.

## What is Qigong?

From the above discussion you can see that Qi is energy, and is found in heaven, in the earth, and in every living thing. All of these different types of energy interact with each other, and can convert into each other. In China, the word "Gong" (or Kung) is often used interchangeably with "Gongfu" (or Kung Fu), which means energy and time. Any study or training which requires a lot of energy and time to learn or to accomplish is called Gongfu. The term can be applied to any special skill or study as long as it requires time, energy, and patience. Therefore, the correct definition of Qigong is any training or study dealing with Qi which takes a long time and a lot of effort.

As stated in the previous section Qi exists in everything, from the largest to the smallest. You can see from that section that Human Qi is part of Heaven and Earth Qi. However, since the human beings who research Qi are mainly interested in Human Qi, the term Qigong is usually used to refer only to Qi training for people.

Qigong research theoretically should include Heaven Qi, Earth Qi, and Human Qi. Understanding Heaven Qi is very difficult. The major rules and principles relating to Heaven Qi can be found in such books as The Five Elements and Ten Stems, Celestial Stems, and the Yi Jing.

Many people have become proficient in the study of Earth Qi. They are called Di Li Shi (Geomancy Teachers) or Feng Shui Shi (Wind Water Teachers). These experts use the accumulated body of geomantic knowledge and the Yi Jing to help people make important decisions such as where and how to build a house, or even where to locate a grave. Teachers in this profession are still quite common in China.

The Chinese people believe that Human Qi is affected and controlled by Heaven Qi and Earth Qi, and that they in fact determine your destiny. Some people specialize in explaining these connections; they are called Suan Ming Shi (Calculate Life Teachers), or fortune tellers.

In any case, most Qigong research has focused on Human Qi. Since Qi is the source of life, if you understand how Qi functions and know how to affect it correctly, you should be able to live a long and healthy life. Many different ways of working with Human Qi have been researched. Acupuncture, acupressure, massage, and herbal treatment have become the root of Chinese medicine. Meditation and moving Qigong exercises are widely used by the Chinese people to improve their health or even to cure certain illnesses. Meditation and Qigong exercises serve an additional role in that Daoists (or Taoists) and Buddhists use them in their spiritual pursuit of enlightenment and Buddhahood.

You can see from this overview that the study of any of the aspects of Qi could be called Qigong. However, since the term is usually used today only in reference to the cultivation of Human Qi, we will use it only in this narrower sense to avoid confusion.

## 1-3. A Brief History of Qigong

The history of Chinese Qigong can be roughly divided into four periods. We know little about the first period, which is considered to have started when the "Yi Jing" (Book of Changes) was introduced sometime before 1122 B.C., and to have extended until the Han dynasty (206 B.C.) when Buddhism and its meditation methods were imported from India. This infusion brought Qigong practice and meditation into the second period, the religious Qigong era. This period lasted until the Liang dynasty (502-557 A.D.), when it was discovered that Qigong could be used for martial purposes. This was the beginning of the third period, that of martial Qigong. Many different martial Qigong styles were created based on the theories and principles of Buddhist and Daoist Qigong. This period lasted until the overthrow of the Qing dynasty in 1911; from that point Chinese Qigong training was mixed with Qigong practices from India, Japan, and many other countries.

### Before the Han Dynasty (Before 206 B.C.)

The "Yi Jing" (Book of Changes; 1122 B.C.) was probably the first Chinese book related to Qi. It introduced the concept of the three natural energies or powers (San Cai): Tian (Heaven), Di (Earth), and Ren (Man). Studying the relationship of these three natural powers was the first step in the development of Qigong.

In 1766-1154 B.C. (the Shang dynasty), the Chinese capital was located in today's An Yang in Henan province. An archeological dig there at a late Shang dynasty burial ground called Yin Xu discovered more than 160,000 pieces of turtle shell and animal bone which were covered with written characters. This writing, called "Jia Gu Wen" (Oracle-Bone Scripture), was the earliest evidence of the Chinese use of the written word. Most of the information recorded was of a religious nature. There was no mention of acupuncture or other medical knowledge, even though it was recorded in the Nei Jing that during the reign of the Yellow emperor (2690-2590 B.C.) Bian Shi (stone probes) were already being used to adjust people's Qi circulation.

During the Zhou dynasty (1122-934 B.C.), Lao Zi (Li Er) mentioned certain breathing techniques in his classic "Dao De Jing" (or Tao Te Ching) (Classic on the Virtue of the Dao). He stressed that the way to obtain health was to "concentrate on Qi and achieve softness" (Zhuan Qi Zhi Rou).(*1) Later, "Shi Ji" (Historical Record) in the Spring and Autumn and Warring States Periods (770-221

B.C.) also described more complete methods of breath training. About 300 B.C. the Daoist philosopher Zhuang Zi described the relationship between health and the breath in his book "Nan Hua Jing." It states: "The men of old breathed clear down to their heels..." This was not merely a figure of speech, and confirms that a breathing method for Qi circulation was being used by some Daoists at that time.

During the Qin and Han dynasties (221 B.C.-220 A.D.) there are several medical references to Qigong in the literature, such as the "Nan Jing" (Classic on Disorders) by the famous physician Bian Que, which describes using the breathing to increase Qi circulation. "Jin Kui Yao Lue" (Prescriptions from the Golden Chamber) by Zhang Zhong-Jing discusses the use of breathing and acupuncture to maintain good Qi flow. "Zhou Yi Can Tong Qi" (A Comparative Study of the Zhou (dynasty) Book of Changes) by Wei Bo-Yang explains the relationship of human beings to nature's forces and Qi. It can be seen from this list that up to this time, almost all of the Qigong publications were written by scholars such as Lao Zi and Zhuang Zi, or physicians such as Bian Que and Wei Bo-Yang.

## From the Han Dynasty to the Beginning of the Liang Dynasty (206 B.C.-502 A.D.)

Because many Han emperors were intelligent and wise, the Han dynasty was a glorious and peaceful period. It was during the Eastern Han dynasty (c. 58 A.D.) that Buddhism was imported to China from India. The Han emperor became a sincere Buddhist; Buddhism soon spread and became very popular. Many Buddhist meditation and Qigong practices, which had been practiced in India for thousands of years, were absorbed into the Chinese culture. The Buddhist temples taught many Qigong practices, especially the still meditation of Chan (Zen), which marked a new era of Chinese Qigong. Much of the deeper Qigong theory and practices which had been developed in India were brought to China. Unfortunately, since the training was directed at attaining Buddhahood, the training practices and theory were recorded in the Buddhist bibles and kept secret. For hundreds of years the religious Qigong training was never taught to laymen. Only in this century has it been available to the general populace.

Not long after Buddhism had been imported into China, a Daoist by the name of Zhang Dao-Ling combined the traditional Daoist principles with Buddhism and created a religion called Dao Jiao. Many of the meditation methods were a combination of the principles and training methods of both sources.

Since Tibet had developed its own branch of Buddhism with its own training system and methods of attaining Buddhahood, Tibetan Buddhists were also invited to China to preach. In time, their practices were also absorbed.

It was in this period that the traditional Chinese Qigong practitioners finally had a chance to compare their arts with the religious Qigong practices imported mainly from India. While the scholarly and medical Qigong had been concerned with maintaining and improving health, the newly imported religious Qigong was concerned with far more. Contemporary documents and Qigong styles show clearly that the religious practitioners trained their Qi to a much deeper level, working with many internal functions of the body, and strove to obtain control of their bodies, minds, and spirits with the goal of escaping from the cycle of reincarnation.

While the Qigong practices and meditations were being passed down secretly within the monasteries, traditional scholars and physicians continued their Qigong research. During the Jin dynasty in the 3rd century A.D., a famous physician named Hua Tuo used acupuncture for anesthesia in surgery. The Daoist Jun Qian used the movements of animals to create the Wu Qin Xi (Five Animal Sports), which taught people how to increase their Qi circulation through specific movements. Also, in this period a physician named Ge Hong mentioned in his book Bao Pu Zi using the mind to lead and increase Qi. Sometime in the period of 420 to 581 A.D. Tao Hong-Jing compiled the "Yang Shen Yan Ming Lu" (Records of Nourishing the Body and Extending Life), which showed many Qigong techniques.

**From the Liang Dynasty to the End of the Qing Dynasty (502-1911 A.D.)**

During the Liang dynasty (502-557 A.D.) the emperor invited a Buddhist monk named Da Mo, who was once an Indian prince, to preach Buddhism in China. The emperor decided he did not like Da Mo's Buddhist theory, so the monk withdrew to the Shaolin Temple. When Da Mo arrived, he saw that the priests were weak and sickly, so he shut himself away to ponder the problem. He emerged after nine years of seclusion and wrote two classics: "Yi Jin Jing" (or Yi Gin Ching)(Muscle/Tendon Changing Classic) and "Xi Sui Jing" (or Shii Soei Ching)(Marrow/Brain Washing Classic). The Muscle/Tendon Changing Classic taught the priests how to gain health and change their physical bodies from weak to strong. The Marrow/Brain Washing Classic taught the priests how to use Qi to clean the bone marrow and strengthen the blood and immune system, as well as how to energize the brain and attain enlightenment. Because the Marrow/Brain Washing Classic was harder to understand and practice, the training methods were passed down secretly to only a very few disciples in each generation.

After the priests practiced the Muscle/Tendon Changing exercises, they found that not only did they improve their health, but they also greatly increased their strength. When this training was integrated into the martial arts forms, it increased the effectiveness of their techniques. In addition to this martial Qigong training, the Shaolin priests also created five animal styles of Gongfu which imitated the way different animals fight. The animals imitated were the tiger, leopard, dragon, snake, and crane.

Outside of the monastery, the development of Qigong continued during the Sui and Tang dynasties (581-907 A.D.). Chao Yuan-Fang compiled the "Zhu Bing Yuan Hou Lun" (Thesis on the Origins and Symptoms of Various Diseases), which is a veritable encyclopedia of Qigong methods listing 260 different ways of increasing the Qi flow. The "Qian Jin Fang" (Thousand Gold Prescriptions) by Sun Si-Mao described the method of leading Qi, and also described the use of the Six Sounds. The Buddhists and Daoists had already been using the Six Sounds to regulate Qi in the internal organs for some time. Sun Si-Mao also introduced a massage system called Lao Zi's 49 Massage Techniques. "Wai Tai Mi Yao" (The Extra Important Secret) by Wang Tao discussed the use of breathing and herbal therapies for disorders of Qi circulation.

During the Song, Jin, and Yuan dynasties (960-1368 A.D.), "Yang Shen Jue" (Life Nourishing Secrets) by Zhang An-Dao discussed several Qigong practices. "Ru Men Shi Shi" (The Confucian Point of View) by Zhang Zi-He describes the use of Qigong to cure external injuries such as cuts and sprains. "Lan Shi Mi Cang" (Secret Library of the Orchid Room) by Li Guo describes using Qigong and herbal remedies for internal disorders. "Ge Zhi Yu Lun" (A Further Thesis of Complete Study) by Zhu Dan-Xi provided a theoretical explanation for the use of Qigong in curing disease.

During the Song dynasty (960-1279 A.D.), Chang San-Feng is believed to have created Taijiquan (or Tai Chi Chuan). Taiji followed a different approach in its use of Qigong than did Shaolin. While Shaolin emphasized Wai Dan (External Elixir) Qigong exercises, Taiji emphasized Nei Dan (Internal Elixir) Qigong training.

In 1026 A.D. the famous brass man of acupuncture was designed and built by Dr. Wang Wei-Yi. Before that time, the many publications which discussed acupuncture theory, principles, and treatment techniques disagreed with each other, and left many points unclear. When Dr. Wang built his brass man, he also wrote a book called "Tong Ren Yu Xue Zhen Jiu Tu" (Illustration of the Brass Man Acupuncture and Moxibustion). He explained the relationship of the 12 organs and the 12 Qi channels, clarified many of the points of confusion, and, for the first time, systematically organized acupuncture theory and principles.

In 1034 A.D. Dr. Wang used acupuncture to cure the emperor Ren Zong. With the support of the emperor, acupuncture flourished. In order to encourage acupuncture medical research, the emperor built a temple to Bian Que, who wrote the Nan Jing, and worshiped him as the ancestor of acupuncture. Acupuncture technology developed so much that even the Jin race in the distant North requested the brass man and other acupuncture technology as a condition for peace. Between 1102 to 1106 A.D. Dr. Wang dissected the bodies of prisoners and added more information to the Nan Jing. His work contributed greatly to the advancement of Qigong and Chinese medicine by giving a clear and systematic idea of the circulation of Qi in the human body.

Later, in the Southern Song dynasty (1127-1279 A.D.), Marshal Yue Fei was credited with creating several internal Qigong exercises and martial arts. It is said that he created the Eight Pieces of Brocade to improve the health of his soldiers. He is also known as the creator of the internal martial style Xing Yi. Eagle style martial artists also claim that Yue Fei was the creator of their style.

From then until the end of the Qing dynasty (1911 A.D.), many other Qigong styles were founded. The well known ones include Hu Bu Gong (Tiger Step Gong), Shi Er Zhuang (Twelve Postures) and Jiao Hua Gong (Beggar Gong). Also in this period, many documents related to Qigong were published, such as "Bao Shen Mi Yao" (The Secret Important Document of Body Protection) by Cao Yuan-Bai, which described moving and stationary Qigong practices; and "Yang Shen Fu Yu" (Brief Introduction to Nourishing the Body) by Chen Ji-Ru, about the three treasures: Jing (essence), Qi (internal energy), and Shen (spirit). Also, "Yi Fan Ji Jie" (The Total Introduction to Medical Prescriptions) by Wang Fan-An reviewed and summarized the previously published materials; and "Nei Gong Tu Shuo" (Illustrated Explanation of Nei Gong) by Wang Zu-Yuan presented the Twelve Pieces of Brocade and explained the idea of combining both moving and stationary Qigong.

In the late Ming dynasty (around 1640 A.D.), a martial Qigong style, Huo Long Gong (Fire Dragon Gong), was created by the Taiyang martial stylists. The well known internal martial art style Ba Gua Zhang (or Ba Kua Chang)(Eight Trigrams Palm) is believed to have been created by Dong Hai-Chuan late in the Qing dynasty (1644-1911 A.D.). This style is now gaining in popularity throughout the world.

During the Qing dynasty, Tibetan meditation and martial techniques became widespread in China for the first time. This was due to the encouragement and interest of the Manchurian Emperors in the royal palace, as well as others of high rank in society.

**From the End of Qing Dynasty to the Present**

Before 1911 A.D., Chinese society was very conservative and old-fashioned. Even though China had been expanding its contact with the outside world for the previous hundred years, the outside world had little influence beyond the coastal regions. With the overthrow of the Qing dynasty in 1911 and the founding of the Chinese Republic, the nation began changing as never before. Since this time Qigong practice has entered a new era. Because of the ease of communication in the modern world, Western culture now has great influence on the Orient. Many Chinese have opened their minds and changed their traditional ideas, especially in Taiwan and Hong Kong. Various Qigong styles are now being taught openly, and many formerly secret documents are being published. Modern methods of communication have opened up Qigong to a much wider audience than ever before, and people now have the opportunity to study and understand many different styles. In addition, people are now able to compare Chinese Qigong to similar arts from other countries such as India, Japan, Korea, and the Middle East.

I believe that in the near future Qigong will be considered the most exciting and challenging field of research. It is an ancient science just waiting to be investigated with the help of the new technologies now being developed at an almost explosive rate. Anything we can do to accelerate this research will greatly help humanity to understand and improve itself.

## 1-4. Categories of Qigong

Generally speaking, all Qigong practices can be divided according to their training theory and methods into two general categories: Wai Dan (External Elixir) and Nei Dan (Internal Elixir). Understanding the differences between them will give you an overview of most Chinese Qigong practices.

### 1.  Wai Dan (External Elixir)

"Wai" means "external or outside," and "Dan" means "elixir." External here means the limbs, as opposed to the torso, which includes all of the vital organs. Elixir is a hypothetical, life-prolonging substance for which Chinese Daoists have been searching for millennia. They originally thought that the elixir was something physical which could be prepared from herbs or chemicals purified in a furnace. After thousands of years of study and experimentation, they found that the elixir is in the body. In other words, if you want to prolong your life, you must find the elixir in your body, and then learn to protect and nourish it.

In Wai Dan Qigong practice, attention is concentrated on the limbs so that the exercise builds up Qi there. When the Qi potential builds to a high enough level, the Qi will flow through the channels, clearing any obstructions and nourishing the organs. This is the main reason that a person who works out, or has a physical job, is generally healthier than someone who sits around all day.

### 2.  Nei Dan (Internal Elixir)

Nei means internal and Dan means elixir. Thus, Nei Dan means to build the elixir internally. Here, internally means in the body instead of in the limbs. Whereas in Wai Dan the Qi is built up in the limbs and then moved into the body, Nei Dan exercises build up Qi in the body and lead it out to the limbs.

Generally speaking, Nei Dan theory is deeper than Wai Dan theory, and its training is more difficult to understand and practice. Traditionally, most of the Nei Dan Qigong practices have been passed down more secretly than those of the Wai Dan. This is especially true of the highest levels of Nei Dan, such as Marrow/Brain Washing, which were passed down to only a few trusted disciples.

We can also classify Qigong into four major categories according to the purpose or final goal of the training: 1. maintaining health; 2.

curing sickness; 3. martial skill; and 4. enlightenment or Buddhahood. This breakdown is only a crude one, however, since almost every style of Qigong serves more than one of the above purposes. For example, although martial Qigong focuses on increasing fighting effectiveness, it can also improve your health. The Daoist Qigong aims for longevity and enlightenment, but to reach this goal you need to be in good health and know how to cure sickness. Because of this multiplicity of functions, we will examine the categories in terms of their backgrounds rather than the goals of their training. Knowing the history and basic principles of each category will help you to understand their Qigong more clearly.

## 1. Scholar Qigong - for Maintaining Health

In China before the Han dynasty, there were two major schools of scholarship. One of them was created by Confucius (551-479 B.C.) during the Spring and Autumn Period; the scholars who practice his philosophy are commonly called Confucians. Later, his philosophy was popularized and enlarged by Mencius (372-289 B.C.) in the Warring States Period. The people who practice this are called Ru Jia (Confucianists). The key words to their basic philosophy are Loyalty, Filial Piety, Humanity, Kindness, Trust, Justice, Harmony, and Peace. Humanity and human feelings are the main subjects of study. Ru Jia philosophy has become the center of much of the Chinese culture.

The second major school of scholarship was called Dao Jia (Daoism or Taoism) and was created by Lao Zi (Lao Tze) in the 6th century B.C. Lao Zi is considered to be the author of a book called the "Dao De Jing" (Morality Classic) which described human morality. Later, in the Warring States Period, his follower Zhuang Zhou wrote a book called "Zhuang Zi," which led to the forming of another strong branch of Daoism (or Taoism). Before the Han dynasty, Daoism was considered a branch of scholarship. However, during the Han dynasty traditional Daoism was combined with the Buddhism imported from India, and it gradually began to be treated as a religion. Therefore, the Daoism before the Han dynasty should be considered scholarly Daoism rather than religious.

In regards to their contribution to Qigong, both schools emphasized maintaining health and preventing disease. They believed that many illnesses are caused by mental and emotional excesses. When a person's mind is not calm, balanced, and peaceful, the organs will not function normally. For example, depression can cause stomach ulcers and indigestion. Anger will cause the liver to malfunction. Sadness will cause stagnation and tightness in the lungs, and fear can disturb the normal functioning of the kidneys and bladder. The scholars realized that if you want to avoid illness, you must learn to balance and relax your thoughts and emotions. This process is called "regulating the mind."

Therefore, the scholars emphasized gaining a peaceful mind through meditation. In their still meditation, the main part of the training consists of getting rid of thoughts so that the mind is clear and calm. When you become calm, the flow of thoughts and emotions slows down, and you feel mentally and emotionally neutral. This kind of meditation can be thought of as practicing emotional self-control. When you are in this "no thought" state, you become very relaxed, and can even relax deep down into your internal organs. When your body is this relaxed, your Qi will naturally flow smoothly and strongly. This kind of still meditation was very common in ancient Chinese scholarly society.

In order to reach the goal of a calm and peaceful mind, the scholars training focused on regulating the mind, body, and breath. They believed that as long as these three things were regulated, the Qi flow would be smooth and sickness would not occur. This is why the Qi training of the scholars is called "Xiu Qi," which means "cultivating Qi." Xiu in Chinese means to regulate, to cultivate, or to repair. It means to maintain in good condition. This is very different from the Daoist Qi training after the Han dynasty which was called "Lian Qi," which is translated "train Qi." Lian means to drill or to practice to make stronger.

Many of the Qigong documents written by the Confucians and Daoists were limited to the maintenance of health. The scholar's attitude in Qigong was to follow his natural destiny and maintain his health. This philosophy is quite different from that of the Daoists after the Han dynasty, who asserted that one's destiny could be changed. They believed that it is possible to train your Qi to make it stronger, and to extend your life. It is said in scholarly society: "Ren Shen Qi Shi Gu Lai Xi,"(*2) which means "in human life seventy is rare." You should understand that few of the common people in ancient times lived past seventy because of the lack of nutritious food and modern medical technology. It is also said: "An Tian Le Ming,"(*3) which means "peace with heaven and delight in your destiny"; and "Xiu Shen Shi Ming,"(*4) which means "cultivate the body and await destiny." Compare this with the philosophy of the later Daoists, who said: "Yi Bai Er Shi Wei Zhi Yao,"(*5) which means "one hundred and twenty means dying young." They believed and have proven that human life can be lengthened and destiny can be resisted and overcome.

Confucianism and Daoism were the two major schools of scholarship in China, but many other schools were also more or less involved in Qigong exercises. We will not discuss them here because there is only a limited number of Qigong documents from these schools.

## 2. Medical Qigong - for Healing

In ancient Chinese society, most emperors respected the scholars and were affected by their philosophy. Physicians, despite having developed a profound and successful medical science, were not regarded highly - indeed, were looked down upon because they made their diagnosis by touching the patient's body, which was considered characteristic of the lower classes in society. However, they continued to work hard and to study, and quietly passed down the results of their research to following generations.

Of all the groups studying Qigong in China, the physicians have pursued the subject for the longest time. Since the discovery of Qi circulation in the human body about four thousand years ago, the Chinese physicians have devoted a major portion of their efforts to studying the behavior of Qi. Their efforts resulted in acupuncture, acupressure or Cavity Press massage, and herbal treatment.

In addition, many Chinese physicians used their medical knowledge to create different sets of Qigong exercises either for maintaining health or for curing specific illnesses. Chinese physicians believed that emulating scholars by doing only sitting or still meditation to regulate the body, mind, and breathing was not enough to cure sickness. They believed that in order to increase the Qi circulation, you must move. Although a calm and peaceful mind was important for health, exercising the body was more important. They learned through their medical practice that people who exercised properly got sick less often, and their bodies degenerated less quickly than was the case with people who just sat around. They also realized that specific body movements could increase the Qi circulation in specific organs. They reasoned from this that Qigong exercises could also be used to treat specific illnesses and to restore the normal functioning of the organs.

Some of these movements (exercises) are similar to - indeed, are modeled on - the way in which certain animals move. It is clear that in order for an animal to survive in the wild, it must have an instinct for how to protect its body. Part of this instinct is concerned with how to build up its Qi, and how to keep its Qi from being lost. We humans have lost many of these instincts over the years that we have been separating ourselves from nature.

A typical, well known set of such exercises is "Wu Qin Xi" (Five Animal Sports) created by Dr. Jun Qian. Another famous set based on similar principles is called "Ba Duan Jin" (The Eight Pieces of Brocade). It was created by Marshal Yue Fei who, interestingly enough, was a soldier rather than a physician.

In addition, using their medical knowledge of Qi circulation, Chinese physicians performed research until they found which movements could help cure particular illnesses and health problems. Not surprisingly, many of these movements were similar to the ones used to maintain health, since many illnesses are caused by unbalanced Qi. When an imbalance continues for a long period of time, the organs will be affected, and may be physically damaged. The situation resembles running a machine without supplying the proper electrical current; over time, the machine will be damaged. Chinese physicians believe that before physical damage to an organ shows up in a patient's body, there is first an abnormality in the Qi balance and circulation. **ABNORMAL QI CIRCULATION IS THE VERY BEGINNING OF ILLNESS AND PHYSICAL ORGAN DAMAGE.**

When Qi is too positive (Yang) or too negative (Yin) in a specific organ's Qi channel, your physical organ is beginning to suffer damage. If you do not correct the Qi circulation, that organ will malfunction or degenerate. The best way to heal someone is to adjust and balance the Qi before there is any physical problem. Therefore, correcting or increasing the normal Qi circulation is the major goal of acupuncture or acupressure treatments. Herbs and special diets are also considered important treatments in regulating the Qi in the body.

As long as the illness is limited to the level of Qi stagnation and there is no physical organ damage, the Qigong exercises used for maintaining health can be used to readjust the Qi circulation and treat the problem. However, if the sickness is already so serious that the physical organs have started to fail, then the situation has become critical and a specific treatment is necessary. The treatment may take the form of acupuncture, herbs, or even an operation, as well as specific Qigong exercises designed to speed up the healing or even to cure the sickness. For example, ulcers and asthma can often be cured or helped by some simple exercises. Recently in both mainland China and Taiwan, Qigong exercises have been shown to be effective in treating certain kinds of cancer.(*6)

Over thousands of years of observing nature and themselves, some Qigong practitioners delved even deeper. They realized that the body's Qi circulation changes with the seasons, and that the body requires help during these periodic adjustments. They noticed also that in each season different organs have characteristic problems. For example, in the beginning of Fall the lungs have to adapt to the colder air that you are breathing. While this adjustment is going on, the lungs are susceptible to disturbance, so your lungs may feel uncomfortable and you may catch colds easily. Your digestive system is also affected during seasonal changes. Your appetite may increase, or you may have diarrhea. When the temperature goes down, your kidneys and bladder will start to give you trouble. For example, because the kidneys are stressed, you may feel pain in the back. Focusing on these seasonal Qi disorders, the meditators created a set of movements which can be used to speed up the body's adjustment. These Qigong exercises will be introduced in a later volume.

In addition to Marshal Yue Fei, many people who were not physicians also created sets of medical Qigong. These sets were probably originally created to maintain health, and later were also used for curing sickness.

### 3. Martial Qigong - for Fighting

Chinese martial Qigong was probably not developed until Da Mo's Muscle/Tendon Changing Classic was developed in the Shaolin Temple during the Liang dynasty (502-557 A.D.). When Shaolin monks trained according to Da Mo's Muscle/Tendon Changing Qigong, they found that they could not only improve their health but also greatly increase the power of their martial techniques. Since then, many martial styles have developed Qigong sets to increase their effectiveness.  In addition, many martial styles have been created based directly on Qigong theory.  Martial artists have thus played a major role in Chinese Qigong development.

When Qigong theory was first applied to the martial arts, it was used to increase the power and efficiency of the muscles.  The theory is very simple - the mind (Yi) is used to lead Qi to the muscles to energize them so that they function more efficiently.  The average person generally uses his muscles at under 40% maximum efficiency.  If one can train in concentration and using a strong Yi (the mind generated from clear thinking) to lead Qi to the muscles effectively, one will be able to energize the muscles to a higher level and, therefore, increase one's fighting effectiveness.

As acupuncture theory became better understood, fighting techniques were able to reach even more advanced levels.  Martial artists learned to attack specific areas, such as vital acupuncture cavities, to disturb the enemy's Qi flow and create imbalances which caused injury or even death.  In order to do this, the practitioner must understand the route and timing of the Qi circulation in the human body.  He also had to train so that he could strike the cavities accurately and to the correct depth.  These cavity strike techniques are called "Dian Xue" (Pointing Cavities) or "Dian Mai" (Dim Mak)(Pointing Vessels).

Most of the martial Qigong practices help to improve the practitioner's health.  However, there are other martial Qigong practices which, although they may build up some special skill which is useful for fighting, also damage the practitioner's health.  An example of this is Iron Sand Palm.  Although this training can build up amazing destructive power, it can also harm your hands and affect the Qi circulation in both the hands and the internal organs.

Since the 6th century, many martial styles have been created which were based on Qigong theory.  They can be roughly divided into external and internal styles.

The external styles emphasize building Qi in the limbs to coordinate with the physical martial techniques.  They follow the theory of Wai Dan (external elixir) Qigong, which usually generates Qi in the limbs through special exercises.  The concentrated mind is used during these exercises to energize the Qi.  This increases muscular strength significantly, and therefore increases the effectiveness of the martial techniques.  Qigong can also be used to train the body to resist punches and kicks.  In this training, Qi is led to energize the skin and the muscles, enabling them to resist a blow without injury.  This training is commonly called "Iron Shirt" (Tie Bu Shan) or "Golden Bell Cover" (Jin Zhong Zhao).  The martial styles which use Wai Dan Qigong training are normally called external styles (Wai Gong) or hard styles (Ying Gong).  Shaolin Gongfu is a typical example of a style which uses Wai Dan martial Qigong.

Although Wai Dan Qigong can help the martial artist increase his power, it has a disadvantage.  Because Wai Dan Qigong emphasizes training the external muscles, it can cause over-development. This can cause a problem called "energy dispersion" (San Gong) when the practitioner grows older. In order to remedy this, when an external martial artist reaches a high level of external Qigong training he will start training internal Qigong, which specializes in curing the energy dispersion problem. That is why it is said "Shaolin Gongfu from external to internal."

Internal Martial Qigong is based on the theory of Nei Dan (internal elixir). In this method, Qi is generated in the body instead of the limbs; this Qi is then led to the limbs to increase power. In order to lead Qi to the limbs, the techniques must be soft and muscle usage must be kept to a minimum. The training and theory of Nei Dan martial Qigong is much more difficult than those of Wai Dan martial Qigong. Interested readers should refer to the author's book: "Advanced Yang Style Tai Chi Chuan - Tai Chi Theory and Tai Chi Jing."

Several internal martial styles were created in the Wudang and E Mei Mountains. Popular styles are Taijiquan (or Tai Chi Chuan), Ba Gua (or Ba Kua), Liu He Ba Fa (or Liu Ho Ba Fa), and Xing Yi (or Hsing Yi). However, you should understand that even the internal martial styles, which are commonly called soft styles, must on some occasions use muscular strength while fighting. Therefore, once an internal martial artist has achieved a degree of competence in internal Qigong, he should also learn how to use harder, more external techniques. That is why it is said: "the internal styles are from soft to hard."

In the last fifty years, some of the Taiji Qigong or Taijiquan practitioners have developed training which is mainly for health, and is called "Wuji Qigong," which means "no extremities Qigong." Wuji is the state of neutrality which precedes Taiji, which is the state of complementary opposites. When there are thoughts and feelings in your mind, there is Yin and Yang; but if you can still your mind, you can return to the emptiness of Wuji. When you achieve this state, your mind is centered and clear, your body relaxed, and your Qi is able to flow naturally and smoothly, reaching the proper balance by itself. Wuji Qigong has become very popular in many parts of China, especially Shanghai and Canton.

You can see that, although Qigong is widely studied in Chinese martial society, the main focus of training was originally the goal of increasing fighting ability rather than health. Good health was considered a by-product of the training. It was not until this century that the health aspect of martial Qigong began to receive greater attention. This is especially true in the internal martial arts. Please refer to the future YMAA in-depth Qigong book series: "Qigong and Martial Arts."

## 4. Religious Qigong - for Enlightenment or Buddhahood

Religious Qigong, though not as popular as other categories in China, is recognized as having achieved the highest accomplishments of all the Qigong categories. This subject used to be kept secret; only in this century has it has been revealed to laymen.

In China, religious Qigong includes mainly Daoist and Buddhist Qigong. The main purpose of their training is striving for enlightenment, or what the Buddhists refer to as Buddhahood. They seek to lift themselves above normal human suffering, and to escape from the cycle of continual reincarnation. They believe that all human suffering is caused by the seven emotions and six desires. If you are still bound to these emotions and desires, you will reincarnate after your death. To avoid reincarnation, you must train your spirit to reach a very high stage where it is strong enough to be independent after your death. This spirit will enter the heavenly kingdom and gain eternal peace. This goal is hard to achieve in the everyday world, so practitioners frequently flee society and move into the solitude of the mountains, where they can concentrate all of their energies on self-cultivation.

Religious Qigong practitioners train to strengthen their internal Qi to nourish their spirit (Shen) until this spirit is able to survive the death of the physical body. Marrow/Brain Washing Qigong training is necessary to reach this stage. It enables them to lead Qi to the forehead, where the spirit resides, and raise the brain to a higher energy state. This training used to be restricted to only a few priests who had reached an advanced level. Tibetan Buddhists were also involved heavily in this training. Over the last two thousand years the Tibetan Buddhists, the Chinese Buddhists, and the Daoists have followed the same principles; they now constitute the three major religious schools of Qigong training.

This religious striving toward enlightenment or Buddhahood is recognized as the highest and most difficult level of Qigong. Many Qigong practitioners rejected the rigors of this religious striving, and practiced Marrow/Brain Washing Qigong solely for the purpose of longevity. It was these people who eventually revealed the secrets of Marrow/Brain Washing to the outside world. If you are interested in knowing more about this training, you may refer to: "Muscle/Tendon Changing and Marrow/Brain Washing Chi Kung" by this author.

## 1-5. Qigong Theory

Many people think that Qigong is a difficult subject to understand. In some ways, this is true. However, you must understand one thing: regardless of how difficult the Qigong theory and practice of a particular style are, the basic theory and principles are very simple and remain the same for all of the Qigong styles. The basic theory and principles are the roots of the entire Qigong practice. If you understand these roots, you will be able to grasp the key to the practice and grow. All of the Qigong styles originated from these roots, but each one has blossomed differently.

In this section we will discuss these basic theories and principles. With this knowledge as a foundation, you will be able to understand not only what you should be doing, but also why you are doing it. Naturally, it is impossible to discuss all of the basic Qigong ideas in such a short section. However, it will offer beginners the key to open the gate into the spacious, four thousand year old garden of Chinese Qigong. If you wish to know more about the theory of Qigong, please refer to: "The Root of Chinese Chi Kung" by this author.

**Qi and Man**

In order to use Qigong to maintain and improve your health, you must know that there is Qi in your body, and you must understand how it circulates and what you can do to insure that the circulation is smooth and strong.

You know from previous discussions that Qi is energy. It is a requirement for life. The Qi in your body cannot be seen, but it can be felt. This Qi can make your body feel too positive (too Yang) or too negative (too Yin).

Imagine that your physical body is a machine, and your Qi is the current that makes it run. Without the current the machine is dead and unable to function. For example, when you pinch yourself, you feel pain. Have you ever thought "how do I feel pain?" You might answer that it is because you have a nervous system in your body which perceives the pinch and sends a signal to the brain. However, there is more to it than that. The nervous system is material, and if it didn't have energy circulating in it, it wouldn't function. Qi is the energy which makes the nervous system and the other parts of your body work. When you pinch your skin, that area is stimulated and the Qi field is disturbed. Your brain is designed to sense this and other disturbances, and to interpret the cause.

According to Chinese Qigong and medicine, the Qi in your body is divided into two categories: Managing Qi (Ying Qi)(which is often called Nutritive Qi) and Guardian Qi (Wei Qi). The Managing Qi is the energy which has been sent to the organs so that they can function. The Guardian Qi is the energy which has been sent to the surface of the body to form a shield to protect you from negative outside influences such as cold. In order to keep yourself healthy, you must learn how to manage these two types of Qi efficiently so they can serve you well.

Qi is classified as Yin because it can only be felt, while the physical body is classified as Yang because it can be seen. Yin is the root and source of the life which animates the Yang body (physical body) and manifests power or strength externally. Therefore, when the Qi is strong, the physical body can function properly and be healthy, and can manifest great power or strength.

In order to have a strong and healthy body, you must learn how to keep the Qi circulating in your body smoothly, and you must also learn how to build up an abundant store of Qi. In order to reach these two goals, you must first understand the Qi circulatory and storage system in your body.

Chinese physicians discovered long ago that the human body has twelve major channels and eight vessels through which the Qi circulates. The twelve channels are like rivers which distribute Qi throughout the body, and also connect the extremities (fingers and toes) to the internal organs. I would like to point out here that the "internal organs" of Chinese medicine do not necessarily correspond to the physical organs as understood in the West, but rather to a set of clinical functions similar to each other, and related to the organ system. The eight vessels, which are often referred to as the extraordinary vessels, function like reservoirs and regulate the distribution and circulation of Qi in your body.

When the Qi in the eight reservoirs is full and strong, the Qi in the rivers is strong and will be regulated efficiently. When stagnation occurs in any of these twelve channels or rivers, the Qi which flows to the body's extremities and to the internal organs will be abnormal, and illness may develop. You should understand that every channel has its particular basic Qi flow strength, and every channel is different. All these different levels of Qi strength are affected by your mind, the weather, the time of day, the food you have eaten, and even your mood. For example, when the weather is dry the Qi in the lungs will tend to be more positive than when it is moist. When you are angry, the Qi flow in your liver channel will be abnormal. The Qi strength in the different channels varies throughout the day in a regular cycle, and at any particular time one channel is strongest. For example, between 11 AM and 1 PM the Qi flow in the heart channel is the strongest. Furthermore, the Qi level of the same organ can be different from one person to another.

Whenever the Qi flow in the twelve rivers or channels is not normal, the eight reservoirs will regulate the Qi flow and bring it back to normal. For example, when you experience a sudden shock, the Qi flow in the bladder immediately becomes deficient. Normally the reservoir will immediately regulate the Qi in this channel so that you recover from the shock. However, if the reservoir Qi is also deficient, or if the effect of the shock is too great and there is not enough time to regulate the Qi, the bladder will suddenly contract, causing unavoidable urination.

When a person is sick because of an injury, his Qi level tends to be either too positive (excessive, Yang) or too negative (deficient, Yin). A Chinese physician either would use a prescription of herbs to adjust the Qi, or else would insert acupuncture needles at various points on the channels to inhibit the flow in some channels and stimulate the flow in others, so that balance can be restored. However, there is another alternative: to use certain physical and mental exercises to adjust the Qi. In other words, to use Qigong.

In the last twenty years, Western medicine has gradually begun to accept the existence of Qi and its circulation in the human body. Several studies indicate that what the Chinese call "Qi" is the bioelectric circulation in the body. It is now generally accepted by Western medicine that an imbalance of the bioelectric current is a major cause of most illness. Modern science is now learning many things which will help us to better understand

Qigong, and will also increase Western medicine's willingness to accept the validity of Qigong.

If Qi is the bioelectricity circulating in the human body, then in order to maintain the circulation of Qi or bioelectricity there must be an EMF (electromagnetic force) generating an electric potential difference. It is like an electric circuit, which must be hooked up to a battery or other source of EMF before there can be a current.

There are two main purposes in Qigong training: first, to maintain the smooth circulation of Qi (bioelectricity), and second, to fill up the Qi vessels (Qi reservoirs) with Qi. In order to have smooth circulation of Qi we must regulate the electric potential difference which controls the Qi flow, and also remove all sources of resistance in the path of the circulation. In order to fill up the Qi vessels, we need to know how to increase the charge in our "battery."

At this point you may ask, "If we keep increasing the EMF of the battery (Qi reservoirs), won't the excess Qi flow overheat the circuit (make it too Yang)?" The answer is yes, this can happen. However, your body is different from a regular electric circuit in that it is alive and can change. When the Qi flow becomes stronger, your body will react and build itself up so that it can accept this new Qi flow. Qigong should be trained slowly and carefully so that, as you build up the Qi stored in your channels, your body has time to readjust itself. This process also makes your body stronger and healthier.

You can see that the key to Qigong practice is, in addition to removing resistance from the Qi channels, maintaining or increasing the Qi level (EMF) in the Qi reservoirs (battery). What are the energy sources in our daily life which supply energy to our body, or, expressed differently, what are the sources by which the EMF can be increased in the body's bioelectric circuit, which would increase the flow of bioelectricity? There are four major sources.

1. **Natural Energy.** Since your body consists of electrically conductive material, its electromagnetic field is always affected by the sun, the moon, clouds, the earth's magnetic field, and by the other energy around you. These affect your Qi circulation significantly, and are responsible for the pattern of your Qi circulation since you were formed. We are now also being greatly affected by energy generated by modern technology, such as radio, TV, microwave ovens, and many other things.

2. **Food and Air.** In order to maintain life, we take in food and air essence through the mouth and nose. These essences are then converted into Qi through a biochemical reaction in the chest and digestive system (called Triple Burners in Chinese medicine). When the Qi is converted from the essence, EMF is generated and circulates the Qi throughout the body. A major part of Qigong is devoted to getting the proper kinds of food and fresh air.

3. **Thinking.** The human mind is the most important and efficient source of bioelectric EMF. Any time you move to do something you must first generate an idea (Yi). This idea

generates the EMF and leads the Qi to energize the appropriate muscles to carry out the desired motion. The more you can concentrate, the stronger the EMF you can generate, and the stronger the flow of Qi you can lead. Naturally, the stronger the flow of Qi you lead to the muscles, the more they will be energized. Because of this, the mind is considered the most important factor in Qigong training.

4. **Exercise.** Exercise converts the food essence (fat) stored in your body into Qi, and therefore builds up the EMF. Many Qigong styles have been created which utilize movement for this purpose.

In Taiji Qigong, the mind and the movements are the two major sources of EMF, though the other two sources are also involved. For example, when you practice in the early morning you can absorb energy from the sun. When you meditate facing the south in the evening you align yourself with the earth's magnetic field. It is also advisable to eliminate greasy and other undesirable foods from your diet, and, if possible, to practice in the mountains where the air is fresh and clear.

## 1-6. General Concepts of Qigong Training

Before you start your Qigong training, you must first understand the three treasures of life - Jing (essence), Qi (internal energy), and Shen (spirit) - as well as their interrelationship. If you lack this understanding, you are missing the root of Qigong training, as well as the basic idea of Qigong theory. The main goals of Qigong training are to learn how to retain your Jing, strengthen and smooth your Qi flow, and enlighten your Shen. To reach these goals you must learn how to regulate the body (Tiao Shen), regulate the mind (Tiao Xin), regulate the breathing (Tiao Xi), regulate the Qi (Tiao Qi), and regulate the Shen (Tiao Shen).

Regulating the body includes understanding how to find and build the root of the body, as well as the root of the individual forms you are practicing. To build a firm root, you must know how to keep your center, how to balance your body, and most important of all, how to relax so that the Qi can flow.

Regulating the mind involves learning how to keep your mind calm, peaceful, and centered, so that you can judge situations objectively and lead Qi to the desired places. The mind is the main key to success in Qigong practice.

To regulate your breathing, you must learn how to breathe so that your breathing and your mind mutually correspond and cooperate. When you breathe this way, your mind will be able to attain peace more quickly, and therefore concentrate more easily on leading the Qi.

Regulating the Qi is one of the ultimate goals of Qigong practice. In order to regulate your Qi effectively you must first have regulated your body, mind, and breathing. Only then will your mind be clear enough to sense how the Qi is distributed in your body, and understand how to adjust it.

For Buddhist priests, who seek the enlightenment of the Buddha, regulating the Shen is the final goal of Qigong. This enables them to maintain a neutral, objective perspective of life. This perspective is the eternal life of the Buddha. The average Qigong practitioner has lower goals. He raises his Shen in order to increase his concentration and enhance his vitality. This makes it possible for him to lead Qi effectively to his entire body so that it carries out the managing and guarding duties. This process maintains his health and slows down aging.

If you understand these few things you will be able to quickly enter into the field of Qigong. Without attention to all these important elements, your training will be ineffective, and your time will be wasted.

**Three Treasures - Jing, Qi, and Shen**

Before you start any Qigong training you must first understand the three treasures (San Bao): Jing (essence), Qi (internal energy), and Shen (spirit). They are also called the three origins or the three roots (San Yuan), because they are considered the origins and roots of your life. Jing means the essence, the most original and refined part of everything. Jing exists in everything. It represents the most basic part of anything which shows its characteristics. Sperm is called Jing Zi, which means "essence of the Son," because it contains the Jing of the father which is passed on to his son (or daughter) and becomes the son's Jing. Jing is the original source of every living thing, and it determines the nature and characteristics of that thing. It is the root of life.

Qi is the internal energy of your body. As noted, it is like the electricity which passes through a machine to keep it running. Qi comes either from the conversion of the Jing which you have received from your parents, or from the food you eat and the air you breathe.

Shen is the center of your mind, the spirit of your being. It is what makes you human, because animals do not have a Shen. The Shen in your body must be nourished by your Qi or energy. When your Qi is full, your Shen will be enlivened.

These three elements are interrelated in a number of ways. Chinese meditators and Qigong practitioners believe that the body contains two general types of Qi. The first type is called Pre-birth Qi, and it comes from converted Original Jing, which you get from your parents at conception. The second type, which is called Post-birth Qi, is drawn from the Jing of the food and air we take in. When this Qi flows or is led to the brain, it can energize the Shen and soul. This energized and raised Shen is able to lead the Qi throughout the entire body.

Each one of these three elements or treasures has its own root. You must know the roots so that you can strengthen and protect your three treasures.

1.    There are many kinds of Jing which your body requires. Except for the Jing which you inherent from your parents,

which is called Original Jing (Yuan Jing), all other Jings must be obtained from food and air. Among all of these Jings, Original Jing is the most important one. It is the root and the seed of your life, and your basic strength. If your parents were strong and healthy, your Original Jing will be strong and healthy, and you will have a strong foundation on which to grow. The Chinese people believe that in order to stay healthy and live a long life, you must protect and maintain this Jing.

The root of Original Jing (Yuan Jing) before your birth was in your parents. After birth this Original Jing stays in its residence - the kidneys, which are considered the root of your Jing. When you keep this root strong, you will have sufficient Original Jing to supply to your body. Although you cannot increase the amount of Jing you have, Qigong training can improve the quality of your Jing. Qigong can also teach you how to convert your Jing into Original Qi more efficiently, and how to use this Qi effectively.

2.     Qi is converted both from the Jing which you have inherited from your parents and from the Jing which you draw from the food and air you take in. Qi which is converted from the Original Jing which you have inherited is called Original Qi (Yuan Qi).(*7) Just as Original Jing is the most important type of Jing, Original Qi is the most important type of Qi. It is pure and of high quality, while the Qi from food and air may make your body too positive or too negative, depending on how and where you absorb it. When you retain and protect your Original Jing, you will be able to generate Original Qi in a pure, continuous stream. As a Qigong practitioner, you must know how to convert your Original Jing into Original Qi in this manner.

Since your Original Qi comes from your Original Jing, they both have the kidneys for their root. When your kidneys are strong, the Original Jing is strong, and the Original Qi converted from this Original Jing will also be full and strong. This Qi resides in the Lower Dan Tian in your abdomen. Once you learn how to convert your Original Jing, you will be able to supply your body with all the Qi it needs.

3.     Shen is the force which keeps you alive. It has no substance, but it gives expression and appearance to your Jing. Shen is also the control tower for the Qi. When your Shen is strong, your Qi is strong and you can lead it efficiently. The root of Shen (spirit) is your mind (Yi, or intention). When your brain is energized and stimulated, your mind will be more aware and you will be able to concentrate more intensely. Also, your Shen will be raised. Advanced Qigong practitioners believe that your brain must always be sufficiently nourished by your Qi. It is the Qi which keeps your mind clear and concentrated. With an abundant Qi supply, the mind can be energized, and can raise the Shen and enhance your vitality.

The deeper levels of Qigong training include the conversion of Jing into Qi, which is then led to the brain to raise the Shen. This process is called "Fan Jing Bu Nao"(*8) and means "return the Jing to nourish the brain." When Qi is led to the head, it stays at the the Upper Dan Tian (center of forehead), which is the residence of your Shen. Qi and Shen are mutually related. When your Shen is weak, your Qi is weak, and your body will degenerate rapidly. Shen is the headquarters of Qi. Likewise, Qi supports the Shen, energizing it and keeping it sharp, clear, and strong. If the Qi in your body is weak, your Shen will also be weak.

**Qigong Training Theory**

In Qigong training it is important to understand the principle behind everything you are doing. The principle is the root of your practice, and it is this root which brings forth the results you want. The root gives life, while the branches and flowers (results) give only temporary beauty. If you keep the root, you can grow. If you have just branches and flowers, they will die in a short time.

Every Qigong form or practice has its special purpose and theory. If you do not know the purpose and theory, you have lost the root (meaning) of the practice. Therefore, as a Qigong practitioner, you must continue to ponder and practice until you understand the root of every set or form.

Before you start training, you must first understand that all of the training originates in your mind. You must have a clear idea of what you are doing, and your mind must be calm, centered, and balanced. Such a condition also implies that your feeling, sensing, and judgement must be objective and accurate; this requires emotional balance and a clear mind. Achieving these goals demands a lot of hard work, but once you have reached this level you will have built the root of your physical training, and your Yi (mind) will be able to lead your Qi throughout your physical body.

As mentioned previously, Qigong training includes five important elements: regulating the body, regulating the breath, regulating the Yi (mind), regulating the Qi, and regulating the Shen (spirit). These are the foundation of successful Qigong practice. Without this foundation, your understanding of Qigong and your practice will remain superficial.

**1. Regulating the Body (Tiao Shen)**

Regulating the Body is called "Tiao Shen" in Chinese. This means to adjust your body until it is in the most comfortable and relaxed state. This implies that your body must be centered and balanced. If it is not, you will be tense and uneasy, and this will affect the judgement of your Yi and the circulation of your Qi. In Chinese medical society it is said: "(When) shape (body's posture) is not correct, then the Qi will not be smooth. (When) the Qi is not smooth, the Yi (mind) will not be peaceful. (When) the Yi is not peaceful, then the Qi is disordered."(*9)  You should understand that the relaxation of your body originates with your Yi.  Therefore, before you can relax your body, you must first relax or regulate your mind (Yi).  This is called "Shen Xin Ping Heng,"(*10) which means "Body and heart (mind) balanced."  The body and the mind are mutually related.  A relaxed and balanced body helps your Yi to relax and concentrate.  Conversely, when your Yi is at peace and can judge things accurately, your body will be centered, balanced, and relaxed.

## Relaxation

Relaxation is one of the major keys to success in Qigong.  You should remember that **ONLY WHEN YOU ARE RELAXED WILL ALL YOUR QI CHANNELS BE OPEN**.  In order to be relaxed, your Yi must first be relaxed and calm.  When this Yi is coordinated with your breathing, your body will be able to relax.

In Qigong practice there are three levels of relaxation.  The first level is the external physical relaxation, or postural relaxation; this is a very superficial level, and almost anyone can reach it.  It consists of adopting a comfortable stance and avoiding unnecessary strain in the manner in which you stand and move.  The second level is the relaxation of the muscles and tendons.  To achieve this your Yi must be directed deep into the muscles and tendons.  This relaxation will help open your Qi channels, and will allow the Qi to sink and accumulate in the Dan Tian.

The final stage is the relaxation which reaches the internal organs and the bone marrow.  Remember, **ONLY IF YOU CAN RELAX DEEP INTO YOUR BODY WILL YOUR MIND BE ABLE TO LEAD THE QI THERE**.  Only at this stage will the Qi be able to reach everywhere.  Then you will feel transparent - as if your whole body had disappeared.  If you can reach this level of relaxation, you will be able to communicate with your organs and use Qigong to adjust or regulate the Qi disorders which are giving you problems.  You will also be able to protect your organs more effectively, and therefore slow down their degeneration.

## Rooting

In all Qigong practice it is very important to be rooted.  Being rooted means to be stable and in firm contact with the ground.  If you want to push a car, you have to be rooted so the force you exert into the car will be balanced by a force into the ground.  If you are not rooted, when you push the car you will only push yourself away, and not move the car.  Your root is made up of your body's root, center, and balance.

Before you can develop your root, you must first relax and let your body "settle."  As you relax, the tension in the various parts of your body will dissolve, and you will find a comfortable way to stand.  You will stop fighting the ground to keep your body up, and will learn to rely on your body's structure to support itself.  This lets the

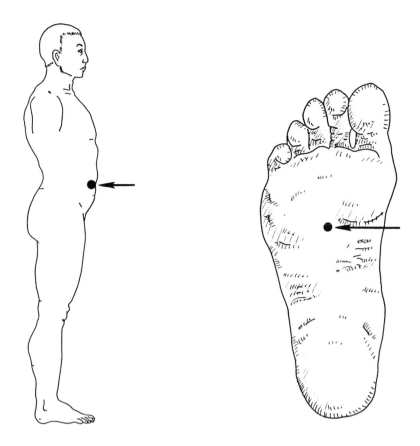

Figure 1-1. Lower Dan Tian

Figure 1-2. Yongquan (or Bubbling Well) cavity (K-1)

muscles relax even more. Since your body isn't struggling to stand up, your Yi won't be pushing upward, and your body, mind, and Qi will all be able to sink. If you let dirty water sit quietly, the impurities will gradually settle down to the bottom, leaving the water above it clear. In the same way, if you relax your body enough to let it settle, your Qi will sink to your Lower Dan Tian (Figure 1-1) and the "Bubbling Wells" cavities in your feet (Figure 1-2), and your mind will become clear. Then you can begin to develop your root.

To root your body you must imitate a tree and grow invisible roots under your feet. This will you stable in your training. **YOUR ROOT MUST BE WIDE AS WELL AS DEEP.** Naturally, your Yi must grow first, because it is the Yi which leads the Qi. Your Yi must be able to lead the Qi to your feet, and be able to communicate with the ground. Only when your Yi can communicate with the ground will your Qi be able to grow beyond your feet and enter the ground to build the root. The Bubbling Well cavity is the gate which enables your Qi to communicate with the ground.

After you have gained your root, you must learn how to keep your center. A stable center will make your Qi develop evenly and uniformly. If you lose this center, your Qi will not be led evenly. In order to keep your body centered, you must first center your Yi, then match your body to it. Only under these conditions will the Qigong forms you practice have their root. Your mental and physical center is the key which enables you to lead your Qi beyond your body.

Balance is the product of rooting and centering. Balance includes balancing the Qi and the physical body. It does not matter which aspect of balance you are dealing with, first you must balance your Yi, and only then can you balance your Qi and your physical body. If your Yi is balanced, it can help you to make accurate judgements, and therefore to correct the path of the Qi flow.

Rooting includes rooting not just the body, but also the form or movement. The root of any form or movement is found in its purpose or principle. For example, in certain Qigong exercises you want to lead the Qi to your palms. In order to do this you must imagine that you are pushing an object forward while keeping your muscles relaxed. In this exercise, your elbows must be down to build the sense of root for the push. If you raise the elbows, you lose the sense of "intention" of the movement, because the push would be ineffective if you were pushing something for real. Since the intention or purpose of the movement is its reason for being, you now have a purposeless movement, and you have no reason to lead Qi in any particular way. Therefore, in this case, the elbow is the root of the movement.

## 2.   Regulating the Breath (Tiao Xi)

Regulating the breath means to regulate your breathing until it is calm, smooth, and peaceful. Only when you have reached this point will you be able to make the breathing deep, slender, long, and soft, which is required for successful Qigong practice.

Breathing is affected by your emotions. For example, when you are angry you exhale more strongly than you inhale. When you are sad, you inhale more strongly than you exhale. When your mind is peaceful and calm, your inhalation and exhalation are relatively equal. In order to keep your breathing calm, peaceful, and steady, your mind and emotions must first be calm and neutral. Therefore, in order to regulate your breathing, you must first regulate your mind.

The other side of the coin is that you can use your breathing to control your Yi. When your breathing is uniform, it is as if you were hypnotizing your Yi, which helps to calm it. You can see that Yi and breathing are interdependent, and that they cooperate with each other. Deep and calm breathing relaxes you and keeps your mind clear. It fills your lungs with plenty of air, so that your brain and entire body have an adequate supply of oxygen. In addition, deep and complete breathing enables the diaphragm to move up and down, which massages and stimulates the internal organs. For this reason, deep breathing exercises are also called "internal organ exercises."

Deep and complete breathing does not mean that you inhale and exhale to the maximum. This would cause the lungs and the surrounding muscles to tense up, which in turn would keep the air from circulating freely, and hinder the absorption of oxygen. Without enough oxygen, your mind becomes scattered, and the rest of your body tenses up. In correct breathing, you inhale and exhale to about 70% or 80% of capacity, so that your lungs stay relaxed.

You can conduct an easy experiment. Inhale deeply so that your lungs are completely full, and time how long you can hold your breath. Then try inhaling to only about 70% of your capacity, and see how long you can hold your breath. You will find that with the latter method you can last much longer than with the first one. This is simply because the lungs and the surrounding muscles are relaxed. When they are relaxed, the rest of your body and your mind can also relax, which significantly decreases your need for oxygen. Therefore, when you regulate your breathing, the first priority is to keep your lungs relaxed and calm.

When training, your mind must first be calm so that your breathing can be regulated. When the breathing is regulated, your mind is able to reach a higher level of calmness. This calmness can again help you to regulate the breathing, until your mind is deep. After you have trained for a long time, your breathing will be full and slender, and your mind will be very clear. It is said: "Xin Xi Xiang Yi,"(*11) which means "Heart (mind) and breathing (are) mutually dependent." When you reach this meditative state, your heartbeat slows down, and your mind is very clear: you have entered the sphere of real meditation.

An Ancient Daoist named Li Qing-An said: "Regulating breathing means to regulate the real breathing until (you) stop."(*12) This means that correct regulating means not regulating. In other words, although you start by consciously regulating your breath, you must get to the point where the regulating happens naturally, and you no longer have to think about it. When you breathe, if you concentrate your mind on your breathing, then it is not true regulating, because the Qi in your lungs will become stagnant. When you reach the level of true regulating, you don't have to pay attention to it, and you can use your mind efficiently to lead the Qi. Remember **WHEREVER THE YI IS, THERE IS THE QI. IF THE YI STOPS IN ONE SPOT, THE QI WILL BE STAGNANT. IT IS THE YI WHICH LEADS THE QI AND MAKES IT MOVE.** Therefore, when you are in a state of correct breath regulation, your mind is free. There is no sound, stagnation, urgency, or hesitation, and you can finally be calm and peaceful.

You can see that when the breath is regulated correctly, the Qi will also be regulated. They are mutually related and cannot be separated. This idea is explained frequently in Daoist literature. The Daoist Guang Cheng Zi said: "One exhale, the Earth Qi rises; one inhale, the Heaven Qi descends; real man's (meaning one who has attained the real Dao) repeated breathing at the navel, then my real Qi is naturally connected."(*13) This says that when you breathe you should move your abdomen, as if you were breathing from your navel. The earth Qi is the negative (Yin) energy from your kidneys, and the sky Qi is the positive (Yang) energy which comes from the food you eat and the air you breathe. When you breathe from the navel, these two Qi's will connect and combine. Many people think that they know what Qi is, but they really don't. Once you connect the two Qi's, you will know what the "real" Qi is, and you may become a "real" human being, which means to attain the Dao.

The Daoist book Chang Dao Zhen Yan (Sing (of the) Dao (with) Real Words) says: "One exhale one inhale to communicate Qi's function, one movement one calmness is the same as (i.e., is the source of) creation and variation."(*14) The first part of this statement again implies that the functioning of Qi is connected with the breathing. The second part of this sentence means that all creation and variation come from the interaction of movement (Yang) and calmness (Yin). Huang Ting Jing (Yellow Yard Classic) says: "Breathe Original Qi to seek immortality."(*15) In China, the traditional Daoists wore yellow robes, and they meditated in a "yard" or hall. This sentence means that in order to reach the goal of immortality, you must seek to find and understand the Original Qi which comes from the Dan Tian through correct breathing.

Moreover, the Daoist Wu Zhen Ren said: "Use the Post-birth breathing to look for the real person's (i.e. the immortal's) breathing place."(*16) In this sentence it is clear that in order to locate the immortal breathing place (the Dan Tian), you must rely on and know how to regulate your Post-birth, or natural, breathing. Through regulating your Post-birth breathing you will gradually be able to locate the residence of the Qi (the Dan Tian), and eventually you will be able to use your Dan Tian to breath like the immortal Daoists. Finally, in the Daoist song Ling Yuan Da Dao Ge (The Great Daoist Song of the Spirit's Origin) it is said: "The Originals (Original Jing, Qi, and Shen) are internally transported peacefully, so that you can become real (immortal); (if you) depend (only) on external breathing (you) will not reach the end (goal)."(*17) From this song, you can see that internal breathing (breathing at the Dan Tian) is the key to training your three treasures and finally reaching immortality. However, you must first know how to regulate your external breathing correctly.

All of these sources emphasize the importance of breathing. There are eight key words for air breathing which a Qigong practitioner should follow during his/her practice. Once you understand them you will be able to substantially shorten the time needed to reach your Qigong goals. These eight key words are: 1. Calm (Jing); 2. Slender (Xi); 3. Deep (Shen); 4. Long (Chang); 5. Continuous (You): 6. Uniform (Yun); 7. Slow (Huan), and 8. Soft (Mian). These key words are self-explanatory, and with a little thought you should be able to understand them.

### 3. Regulating Mind (Tiao Xin)

It is said in Daoist society that: "(When) large Dao is taught, first stop thought; when thought is not stopped, (the lessons are) in vain."(*18) This means that when you first practice Qigong, the most difficult training is to stop your thinking. The final goal for your mind is "the thought of no thought."(*19) Your mind does not think of the past, the present, or the future. Your mind is completely separated from influences of the present such as worry, happiness, and sadness. Then your mind can be calm and steady, and can finally gain peace. Only when you are in the state of "the thought of no thought" will you be relaxed and be able to sense calmly and accurately.

Regulating your mind means using your consciousness to stop the activity in your mind in order to set it free from the bondage of ideas, emotion, and conscious thought. When you reach this level your mind will be calm, peaceful, empty, and light. Then your mind has really reached the goal of relaxation. Only when you reach this stage will you be able to relax deep into your marrow and internal organs. Only then will your mind be clear enough to see (feel) the internal Qi circulation and communicate with your Qi and organs. In Daoist society it is called "Nei Shi Gongfu,"(*20) which means the Gongfu of internal vision.

When you reach this real relaxation you may be able to sense the different elements which make up your body: solid matter, liquids, gases, energy, and spirit. You may even be able to see or feel the different colors that are traditionally associated with your five organs - green (liver), white (lungs), black (kidneys), yellow (spleen), and red (heart).

Once your mind is relaxed and regulated and you can sense your internal organs, you may decide to study the five element theory. This is a very profound subject, and it is sometimes interpreted differently by Oriental physicians and Qigong practitioners. When understood properly, it can give you a method of analyzing the interrelationships between your organs, and help you devise ways to correct imbalances.

For example, the lungs correspond to the element Metal, and the heart to the element Fire. Metal (the lungs) can be used to adjust the heat of the Fire (the heart), because metal can take a large quantity of heat away from fire, (and thus cool down the heart). When you feel uneasy or have heartburn (excess fire in the heart), you may use deep breathing to calm down the uneasy emotions or cool off the heartburn.

Naturally, it will take a lot of practice to reach this level. In the beginning, you should not have any ideas or intentions, because they will make it harder for your mind to relax and empty itself of thoughts. Once you are in a state of "no thought," place your attention on your Dan Tian. It is said "Yi Shou Dan Tian,"(*21) which means "The Mind is kept on the Dan Tian." The Dan Tian is the origin and residence of your Qi. Your mind can build up the Qi here (start the fire, Qi Huo), then lead the Qi anywhere you wish, and finally lead the Qi back to its residence. When your mind is on the Dan Tian, your Qi will always have a root. When you keep this root, your Qi will be strong and full, and it will go where you want it to. You can see that when you practice Qigong, your mind cannot be completely empty and relaxed. You must find the firmness within the relaxation, then you can reach your goal.

In Qigong training, it is said: "Use your Yi (mind) to **LEAD** your Qi" (Yi Yi Yin Qi).(*22) Notice the word **LEAD**. Qi behaves like water - it cannot be pushed, but it can be led. When Qi is led, it will flow smoothly and without stagnation. When it is pushed, it will flood and enter the wrong paths. Remember, wherever your Yi goes first, the Qi will naturally follow. For example, if you intend to lift an object, this intention is your Yi. This Yi will lead the Qi to the arms to energize the physical muscles, and then the object can be lifted.

It is said: "Your Yi cannot be on your Qi. Once your Yi is on your Qi, the Qi is stagnant."(*23) When you want to walk from one spot to another, you must first mobilize your intention and direct it to the goal, then your body will follow. The mind must always be ahead of the body. If your mind stays on your body, you will not be able to move.

In Qigong training, the first thing is to know what Qi is. If you do not know what Qi is, how will you be able to lead it? Once you know what Qi is and experience it, then your Yi will have something to lead. The next thing in Qigong training is knowing how your Yi communicates with your Qi. That means that your Yi should be able to sense and feel the Qi flow and understand how strong and smooth it is. In Taiji Qigong society, it is commonly said that your Yi must "listen" to your Qi and "understand" it. Listen here means to pay careful attention to what you sense and feel. The more you pay attention and increase your awareness, the better you will be able to understand. Only after you understand the Qi situation will your Yi be able to set up the strategy. In Qigong your mind or Yi must generate the idea (visualize your intention), which is like an order to your Qi to complete a certain mission.

The more your Yi communicates with your Qi, the more efficiently the Qi can be led. For this reason, as a Qigong beginner you must first learn about Yi and Qi, and also learn how to help them communicate efficiently. Yi is the key in Qigong practice. Without this Yi you will not be able to lead your Qi, let alone build up the strength of the Qi or circulate it throughout your entire body.

Remember **WHEN THE YI IS STRONG, THE QI IS STRONG, AND WHEN THE YI IS WEAK, THE QI IS WEAK**. Therefore, the first step of Qigong training is to develop your Yi. The first secret of a strong Yi is **CALMNESS**. When you are calm, you can see things clearly and not be disturbed by surrounding distractions. With your mind calm, you will be able to concentrate.

Confucius said: "First you must be calm, then your mind can be steady. Once your mind is steady, then you are at peace. Only when you are at peace are you able to think and finally gain."(*24) This procedure is also applied in meditation or Qigong exercise: First Calm, then Steady, Peace, Think, and finally Gain. When you practice Qigong, first you must learn to be emotionally calm. Once calm, you will be able to see what you want and firm your mind (steady). This firm and steady mind is your intention or Yi (it is how your Yi is generated). Only after you know what you really want will your mind gain peace and be able to relax emotionally and physically. Once you have reached this step, you must then concentrate or think in order to execute your intention. Under this thoughtful condition of a concentrated mind, your Qi will follow and you will be able to gain what you wish.

### 4.   Regulating the Qi (Tiao Qi)

Before you can regulate your Qi you must first regulate your body, breath, and mind. If you compare your body to a battlefield, then your mind is like the general who generates ideas and controls the situation, and your breathing is the strategy. Your Qi is like the soldiers who are led to the most advantageous places on the battlefield. All four elements are necessary, and all four must be coordinated with each other if you are to win the war against sickness and aging.

If you want to arrange your soldiers most effectively for battle, you must know which area of the battlefield is most important, and where you are weakest (where your Qi is deficient) and need to send reinforcements. If you have more soldiers than you need in one area (excessive Qi), then you can send them somewhere else where the ranks are thin. As a general, you must also know how many soldiers are available for the battle, and how many you will need for protecting yourself and your headquarters. To be successful, not only do you need good strategy (breathing), but you also need to communicate with your troops and understand their situation effectively, or all of your strategy will be in vain. When your Yi (the general) knows how to regulate the body (knows the battlefield), how to regulate the breathing (sets up the strategy), and how to effectively regulate the Qi (directs your soldiers), you will be able to reach the final goal of Qigong training.

In order to regulate your Qi so that it moves smoothly in the correct paths, you need more than just efficient Yi-Qi communication. You also need to know how to generate Qi. If you do not have enough Qi in your body, how can you regulate it? In a battle, if you do not have enough soldiers to set up your strategy, you have already lost.

When you practice Qigong, you must first train to make your Qi flow naturally and smoothly. There are some Qigong exercises in which you intentionally hold your Yi, and thus Qi, in a specific area. As a beginner, however, you should first learn how to make the Qi flow smoothly instead of building a Qi dam, which is commonly done in external martial Qigong training.

In order to make Qi flow naturally and smoothly, your Yi must first be relaxed. Only when your Yi is relaxed will your body be relaxed and the Qi channels open for the Qi to circulate. Then you must coordinate your Qi flow with your breathing. Breathing regularly and calmly will make your Yi calm, and allow your body to relax even more.

## 5. Regulating the Spirit (Tiao Shen)

There is one thing that is more important than anything else in a battle, and that is fighting spirit. You may have the best general, who knows the battlefield well and is also an expert strategist, but if his soldiers do not have a high fighting spirit (morale), he might still lose. Remember, **SPIRIT IS THE CENTER AND ROOT OF A FIGHT**. When you keep this center, one soldier can be equal to ten soldiers. When his spirit is high, a soldier will obey his orders accurately and willingly, and his general will be able to control the situation efficiently. In a battle, in order for a soldier to have this kind of morale, he must know why he is fighting, how to fight, and what he can expect after the fight. Under these conditions, he will know what he is doing and why, and this understanding will raise up his spirit, strengthen his will, and increase his patience and endurance.

It is the same with Qigong training. In order to reach the final goal of Qigong you must have three fundamental spiritual roots: will, patience, and endurance.

Shen, which is the Chinese term for spirit, originates from the Yi (the general). When the Shen is strong, the Yi is firm. When the Yi is firm, the Shen will be steady and calm. **THE SHEN IS THE MENTAL PART OF A SOLDIER. WHEN THE SHEN IS HIGH, THE QI IS STRONG AND EASILY DIRECTED. WHEN THE QI IS STRONG, THE SHEN IS ALSO STRONG.**

All of these training concepts and procedures are common to all Chinese Qigong; you should adhere to them also when practicing Taijiquan. To reach a deep level of understanding and penetrate to the essence of any Qigong practice, you should always keep these five training criteria in mind and examine them for deeper levels of meaning. This is the only way to gain the real mental and physical health benefits from your training. Always remember that the essence of Qigong training is not just in the forms. Your feelings and comprehension are the essential roots of the entire training. This Yin side of the training has no limit, and the deeper you understand, the more you will see that there is to know.

## 1-7. How to Use This Book

When you practice any Qigong, you must first ask: What, Why, and How. "What" means: "What am I looking for?" "What do I expect?" and "What should I do?" Then you must ask: "Why do I need it?" "Why does it work?" "Why must I do it this way instead of that way? " Finally, you must determine: "How does it work?" "How much have I advanced toward my goal?" And "How will I be able to advance further?"

It is very important to understand what you are practicing, not just automatically to repeat what you have learned. Understanding is the root of any work. With understanding you will be able to know your goal. Once you know your goal, your mind can be firm and steady. With this understanding, you will be able to see why something has happened, and what the principles and theories behind it are. Without all of this, your work will be done blindly, and it will be a long and painful process. Only when you are sure what your target is and why you need to reach it should you raise the question of how you are going to accomplish it. The answers to all of these questions form the root of your practice, and will help you to avoid the wondering and confusion that uncertainty brings. If you keep this root, you will be able to apply the theory and make it grow - you will know how to create. Without this root, what you learn will be only branches and flowers, and in time they will wither.

In China there is a story about an old man who was able to change a piece of rock into gold. One day, a boy came to see him and asked for his help. The old man said: "Boy! What do you want? Gold? I can give you all of the gold you want." The boy replied: "No, Master, what I want is not your gold. What I want is the trick of how to change the rock into gold!" When you just have gold, you can spend it all and become poor again. If you have the trick of how to make gold, you will never be poor. For the same reason, when you learn Qigong you should learn the theory and principle behind it, not just the practice. Understanding theory and principle will not only shorten your time of pondering and practice, but also enable you to practice most efficiently.

One of the hardest parts of the training process is learning how actually to do the forms correctly. Every Qigong movement has its special meaning and purpose. In order to make sure your movements or forms are correct, it is best to work with the tape and book together. There are some important aspects which you may not be able to pick up from reading, but once you see them, they will be clear. There are other important ideas for which it was impossible to take the time to explain in the videotape, such as the theory and principles; these can only be explained in the book. It cannot be denied that under the tutelage of a master you can learn more quickly and perfectly than is possible using only tapes and books. What you are missing is the master's experience and feeling. However, if you ponder carefully and practice patiently and perseveringly, you will be able to make up for this lack through your own experience and practice. This book and tape are designed for self-instruction. You will find that they will serve you as a key to enter into the field of Qigong.

# References

(*1). 專氣致柔

(*2). 人生七十古來稀

(*3). 安天樂命

(*4). 修身俟命

(*5). 一百二十謂之天

(*6). There are many reports in popular and professional literature of using Qigong to help or even cure many illnesses, including cancer. Many cases have been discussed in the Chinese Qigong journals. One book which describes the use of Qigong to cure cancer is New Qigong for Preventing and Curing Cancer ( 新氣功防治癌症 ), by Ye Ming, Chinese Yoga Publications, Taiwan, 1986.

(*7). Before birth you have no Qi of your own, but rather you use your mother's Qi. When you are born, you start creating Qi from the Original Jing which you received from your parents. This Qi is called Pre-birth Qi, as well as Original Qi. It is also called Pre-heaven Qi (Xian Tian Qi) because it comes from the Original Jing which you received before you saw the heavens (which here means the sky), i.e. before your birth.

(*8). 還精補腦

(*9). 形不正，則氣不順．氣不順，則意不寧．意不寧，則氣散亂．

(*10). 身心平衡

(*11). 心息相依

(*12). 調息要調無息息

(*13). 廣成子曰："一呼則地氣上升，一吸則天氣下降，人之反覆呼吸於蒂，則我之真氣自然相接．"

(*14). 唱道真言曰："一呼一吸通乎氣機，一動一靜同乎造化．"

(*15). 黃庭經曰："呼吸元氣以求仙．"

(*16). 伍真人曰："用後天之呼吸，尋真人之呼吸處．"

(*17). 靈源大道歌曰："元和內運即成真，呼吸外求終未了．"

(*18). 大道教人先止念，念頭不住亦徒然．

(*19). 無念之念

(*20). 內視功夫

(*21). 意守丹田

(*22). 以意引氣

(*23). 意不在氣，在氣則滯．

(*24). 孔子曰："先靜爾後有定，定爾後能安，安爾後能慮，慮爾後能得．"

# Chapter 2
# What is Arthritis?

In this chapter we will first describe arthritis from the point of view of both Western Medicine and Chinese medicine. In the second section we will review the structure of a joint so that you will more easily understand our discussion of the different forms of arthritis in the third section. In the fourth section we will briefly consider the possible causes of arthritis. Finally, in the fifth section we will review other means of preventing or curing arthritis.

## 2-1. What is Arthritis?

Although both the Western and the Chinese systems of medicine describe arthritis in very similar ways, especially in regards to symptoms, there are a number of differences in how the two cultures approach the disease.

### The Western Approach to Arthritis

Before discussing arthritis, we would first like to mention another popular, non-medical term, rheumatism, which is commonly confused with arthritis. Rheumatism has come to mean so many things to so many people that it is almost impossible to give it a clear definition. The term rheumatism commonly refers to any of several pathological conditions of the muscles, tendons, joints, bones, or nerves, characterized by discomfort and disability. This includes variable, shifting, painful inflammation and stiffness of the muscles, joints, or other structures.

The term arthritis is also commonly misused to refer to any vague pain in the area of the joints. However, joints are complicated mechanisms made up of ligaments, tendons, muscles, cartilage, and bursae, and pain in them can have many different causes. Arthritis is specifically an inflammation of the joints. The word arthritis is derived from the Greek words *arthron* (joint) and *itis* (inflammation). Therefore, if you have pain or swelling caused by injury to the ligaments or muscles, you may not classify it as arthritis. You can see that while arthritis is (in a popular sense) a form of rheumatism, rheumatism is not necessarily arthritis.

The symptoms or characteristics of arthritis are pain, swelling, redness, heat, stiffness, and deformity in one or more joints. Arthritis may appear suddenly or gradually, and it may feel different to different people. Some patients feel a sharp, burning, or grinding pain, while others may feel a pain like a toothache. The same person may feel it at some times as pain, and at other times as stiffness. If we look more closely at these signs we can detect certain characteristic physiological changes. These changes include dilation of the blood vessels in the affected area and an increase of blood flow at the site of inflammation. In addition, there is increased permeability in these vessels, as white blood cells, which fight infection, infiltrate the diseased tissue. Finally, fluid from the blood can also leak into the tissue and generate edema or swelling. For these reasons, arthritis may affect not only the joints but also other connective tissues of the body. These tissues include several supporting structures such as muscles, tendons, and ligaments, and the protective coverings of some internal organs.

Depending on where and how the problem started, and on what pathologic process is operating, arthritis can be classified into different forms such as gout, osteoarthritis, rheumatoid arthritis and many others. We will discuss these in the third section.

**The Chinese Approach to Arthritis**

Although the symptoms of arthritis remain the same everywhere, the Chinese physicians consider them from a different point of view. Like all other cases of illness, Chinese physicians diagnose by evaluating the imbalance of Qi (which the West now calls bioelectricity) in the body, as well as by considering the actual physical symptoms.

Chinese medicine has found that, before a physical illness occurs, the Qi becomes unbalanced. If this Qi imbalance is not corrected, the physical body can be damaged and the physical symptoms of sickness will appear. The reason for this is very simple. Every cell in your body is alive, and in order to stay alive and functioning, each requires a constant supply of Qi. Whenever the supply of Qi to the cells becomes irregular (or the Qi "loses its balance"), the cells will start to malfunction. Chinese physicians try to intercept the problem before there is any actual physical damage, and correct the situation with acupuncture, herbal treatments, or a number of other methods. In this way they hope to prevent physical damage, which is considered the worst stage of an illness. Once the physical body, for example an internal organ, has been damaged, it is almost impossible to make a 100% recovery. This approach is the root of Chinese medicine.

Chinese physicians try to diagnose arthritis in its earliest stages, before there is any physical damage. When the Qi starts to become unbalanced, although there are no physical changes, the patient suffers from nerve pain. Because human Qi is strongly affected by the natural Qi present in clouds, moisture, and the sun (both day and night), the body's Qi is easily disturbed by changes in the weather, and arthritis patients will usually feel pain in the joints. When cloud cover is low and there is a lot of moisture in the air, the potential of the earth's electromagnetic field is also increased, and your body's Qi balance can be significantly influenced. The other obvious symptom of this influence is emotional disturbance. In the West, as long as there is no symptom of physical damage, these feelings of physical and emotional pain are usually ignored, although sometimes drugs are prescribed to stop the pain. Although Western physicians sometimes consider this an early stage of arthritis, Chinese physicians do not, and refer to it instead as "Feng Shi," or "wind moisture." This refers to the cause of the pain that the patients feel. Eastern medical dictionaries often translate "Feng Shi" as "rheumatism."

Although countless arthritis patients regularly feel their pain worsen when the weather changes, scientists who conducted studies in an experimental climate chamber at the University of Pennsylvania concluded that there is no evidence that the weather affects arthritis.(*1) I believe that this is solely because Western medicine does not take Qi/bioelectricity into account. When Western medicine starts to understand the relationship between environmental Qi and human Qi, then ample evidence of this association will emerge.

In China, when Feng Shi occurs, people will usually seek out a physician to correct the problem through acupuncture, massage, acupressure, herbal treatment, or Qigong exercises, or most commonly a combination of these methods. The specific treatment would, of course, depend upon the symptoms of each individual case. For example, if the Feng Shi stems from an old joint injury, the treatment will be different than if it were caused by weak joints. The key to treatment is finding the root of the Qi imbalance and correcting it. Only when this root cause is removed will the patient recover completely.

There are many possible causes of Feng Shi. The most common cause is a joint injury which never completely healed, and caused a gradually increasing disturbance of the Qi circulation. Fortunately, if the patient practices the correct Qigong exercises, the joint can be healed completely and its strength rebuilt. Exercise stimulates the Qi and increases its circulation, which removes stagnation and blockages and lets the body's natural healing mechanism operate. Smooth Qi circulation is the root of health and the foundation of healing.

Feng Shi will frequently also be found in patients who were born with weak joints or deformities, such as having one leg significantly longer than the other. Naturally, the most common and serious cases of Feng Shi are caused by aging. As we grow older, the muscles and tendons degenerate and start functioning less effectively around the joints, a process which places more pressure on the cartilage, synovium (joint surface), capsule, and the bones. This is the main cause of arthritis in older people.

If a person with Feng Shi does not seek to correct the problem, or the physician fails to correct it, the Feng Shi may develop into an infectious joint problem (Guan Jie Yan), which is what the Chinese call arthritis, and the joint will begin to suffer physical damage. The indications of an infectious problem are swelling, redness, pain, stiffness, sometimes fever, and deformity of the joint. This stage is already considered serious. Unlike Western medicine, traditional Chinese medicine does not differentiate among the various forms of arthritis, such as gout and osteoarthritis.

Now that you have a general idea of how Western medicine and Chinese medicine approach arthritis, we will review the structure of a joint so that you will gain a clear understanding when we discuss the different forms of arthritis.

### 2-2. The Structure of Joints

It is very important that you understand the different parts which make up a joint, so that we can pinpoint exactly where the problem is.

Generally speaking, a joint is a junction where two bones meet in a way that permits each to move in relation to the other. The human body has 68 joints. Joints are made up of bones, cartilage, capsule, synovium, and ligaments. Covering the joints are tendons, muscles, and skin. Arthritis is associated mainly with cartilage, capsule, synovium, and ligaments, so we will only discuss these parts and how they function.(*1)

1. **Cartilage** (Figure 2-1):
   Cartilage, also called "gristle," is a smooth, glistening, very tough, white fibrous connective tissue attached to the surfaces of bones at the joint. It is a major constituent of the fetal and young vertebrate skeleton; with maturation it is largely converted to bone. Between cartilages is an area called "joint space" or "synovial cavity." This space contains the synovial fluid, which lubricates the cartilage and the joint space to maintain easy movement.

2. **Capsule** (Figure 2-2):
   The capsule is a bag or wrapping of soft tissue which surrounds the cartilage and the joint space. The capsule is usually quite loose, which allows the joint to move easily. Within the bag is a very critical structure called the "synovium."

3. **Synovium** (Figure 2-2):
   The synovium or "synovial membrane" is a wet, velvety, and very delicate lining on the inner surface of the fibrous capsule. It constitutes the actual "sliding surface" of the joint. It manufactures the "synovial fluid," which lubricates the joint, and also removes bits of foreign tissue, bacteria, and other waste matter from the joint space, absorbing them into the cells of the synovial lining and digesting them.

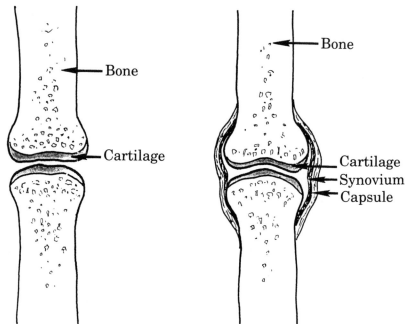

Figure 2-1. Bone, cartilage

Figure 2-2. Bone, cartilage, capsule and synovium

4. **Ligaments** (Figure 2-3):

A ligament is a band or sheet of tough, firm, compact, fibrous tissue, which closely binds the related structures, such as bones, organs, fascia, or muscle together. The purpose of ligaments at the joints is to hold the bones together and keep them in the correct orientation to each other. Ligaments are firm rope-like structures on the outside of the joints. Collagen, a fibrous protein, is an important component of ligaments, and is also part of the structure of bones. Collagen fibers from the ligament extend into the collagen of the bone where the two meet. However, there is a sharp change in the nature of the tissue. Collagen in bone is calcified and still, while in the ligament the collagen is not calcified, so it is relatively flexible, though still firm. Usually, when an ankle is sprained it is the ligament that is torn or damaged, often at the place where it joins the bones.

Now that you have a better understanding of the structure of a joint, let us review the different forms of arthritis and related disorders according to Western medicine.

## 2-3. The Different Forms of Arthritis and Related Disorders

As mentioned previously, Chinese medicine does not differentiate between the various forms of arthritis, as does Western medicine. Western medicine considers arthritis to be not a single disease, but a family of more than 100 separate diseases and disorders. Generally, they are classified according to the cause, the location of the joint

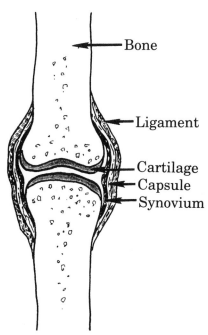

Figure 2-3. Bone, cartilage, capsule, synovium, and ligament

where the arthritis started, and even the age of the patient. This seems to indicate that Western medicine has studied - or at least cataloged - the condition more deeply than have the Chinese. Let us review the most common forms of arthritis, and describe briefly how they are treated by Western medicine.

## 1.   Infectious Arthritis:

Infectious arthritis is generally caused by bacterial infection inside a joint (often called a "septic joint").(*2)  The infected joint is usually painful and may also be swollen.  This form of arthritis can develop from a penetrating wound that damages the joint, or from an injury in the joint area.  In addition, bacteria from various infectious diseases such as tuberculosis, brucellosis, undulant fever and others may reach the joints through the blood stream and attack them.  For example, arthritis can occur because of gonorrhea (a venereal disease with inflammation of the genital organs), in which the germs are carried from the infected, pus-containing genital organs through the blood to the joints.

Treatment with penicillin and other modern antibiotics is usually very successful if started promptly.  Therefore, it is very important to see a physician when a joint hurts or becomes hot, swollen, or reddened; the presence of fever increases the urgency of the need for medical attention.

## 2.   Gout:

Gout, also called "gouty arthritis," is commonly considered to be an illness of the rich which is attributed to high living, rich food, and excessive wine (Figure 2-4).  Medically, gout is considered to be an

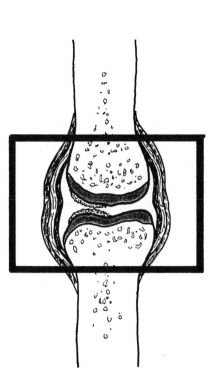

Figure 2-4. Gout

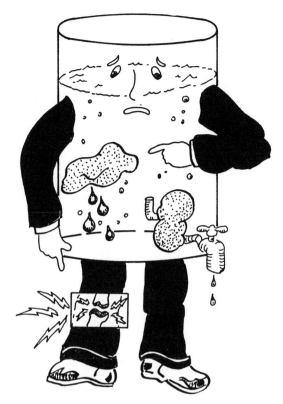

Figure 2-5. Imbalanced function of
liver and kidneys

inherited ailment related to abnormal metabolism, and resulting from the retention of uric acid. Uric acid is a breakdown product of "purines," important compounds which exist in foods such as meat and red wines, so it is a normal ingredient of the diet.

Our bodies manufacture uric acid in the liver. Whenever there is an excessive amount of uric acid, it is excreted mostly through the kidneys. If excretion is slower than production, the level of uric acid in the body can rise. This can result in gout, or in gouty lumps in bone, cartilage, or skin which are called tophi.

When excess uric acid is deposited in the joints, it may result in an inflammatory reaction from the joint tissues which causes severe pain, swelling, and stiffness (Figure 2-5). Gout attacks more men than women, commonly in the lower extremities, especially the big toes. However, any other joint in the body can also be involved (Figure 2-6). If gout is not treated promptly, it can be severe and disabling, and may lead to permanent deformity. In addition, uncontrolled gout can injure the kidneys, usually through the formation of stones.

Gout is a form of arthritis which can be effectively treated.(*1) Although certain foods may precipitate gout attacks, modern medical treatment will usually make it unnecessary to ban many "rich" foods from the diet, with the possible exception of such items as anchovies, sweetbreads, liver, and kidney. In fact, in most cases it was not the rich foods which caused the excess of uric acid in the body.

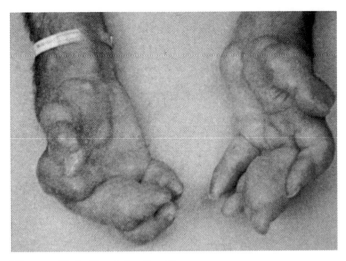

Figure 2-6. Gout in the fingers

Today, excellent medicines are available which can not only relieve the agony of gouty arthritis once an attack has begun, but can also prevent attacks. There are two common ways of preventing the attacks of gout through reducing the body's burden of uric acid. The first way is to block the manufacture of the enzyme that converts materials into uric acid, so that uric acid is not formed. The second way is to facilitate uric acid excretion, and thus reduce the acid level. The regular use of those two methods, either together or separately, can produce gradual dissolution of the tophi and may totally prevent arthritis.

However, when an attack has already started, a drug called "colchicine" can stop the attack, usually within twenty-four hours. Phenylbutazone and other agents may be used once an attack has started.

### 3.  Osteoarthritis:

Osteoarthritis is also called "degenerative joint disease" or "wear and tear" arthritis, and is one of the most common disorders of the human race, especially for those who are getting into old age (Figure 2-7). About 8.7% of the adult population has osteoarthritis, while only about 1% has rheumatoid arthritis. Osteoarthritis rarely develops before a person reaches forty years of age. However, X-rays show that virtually everyone over age 60 has some signs of it. X-rays taken for heart and lung conditions usually also show a touch of arthritis in the spine. However, the majority of people who show osteoarthritis in the the X-rays may never experience the symptoms of aches, pain, or stiffness.

Osteoarthritis is primarily caused by repeated or prolonged microtrauma, or the repeated ignoring of minor joint injuries. When osteoarthritis attacks, it affects the cartilage of the joint, causing it to fray, wear, tear, and ulcerate. In serious cases, cartilage may split, and fragments may fall off and finally disappear entirely, leaving a

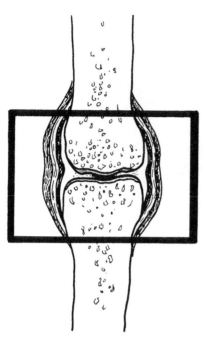

Figure 2-7. Osteoarthritis

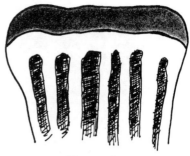

Normal

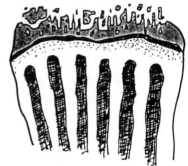

Disease

Figure 2-8. Normal and diseased cartilage

bone-on-bone joint (Figure 2-8). Underneath the diseased portion of
cartilage, bone may proliferate and become hard and dense. When
this happens, spurs or little lumps may form on the bone at the
edges of the joint (Figure 2-9). These symptoms commonly direct
physicians to the diagnosis of osteoarthritis. These lumps usually do
not cause discomfort to the patient.

Osteoarthritis lumps usually appear in the joints of the last
section of the fingers (known as Heberden's nodes)(Figure 2-10). Pain
may occur in the beginning, and then disappear after a few months.
When this occurs, although the remaining lump is disfiguring, the
patient can perform almost any activity without feeling discomfort.

Another common site for osteoarthritis is the neck, often due to
an impact injury. Osteoarthritis also develops frequently in the
lower back, the hips, and the knees. The hips and knees are especially vulnerable to osteoarthritis in overweight people, perhaps due
to the extra weight bearing on the joints. X-rays show that normal
knees have a wide joint space and sharp bone edges (Figure 2-11).
However, in serious cases of osteoarthritis, because of the loss of cartilage the joint space is decreased, and the bone is rough and con-
densed (Figure 2-12).

Although osteoarthritis usually does not result in crippling, disability may occur when severe osteoarthritis occurs in the hip.

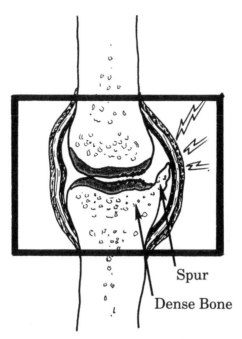

Spur

Dense Bone

Figure 2-9. Spurs can form on the bone

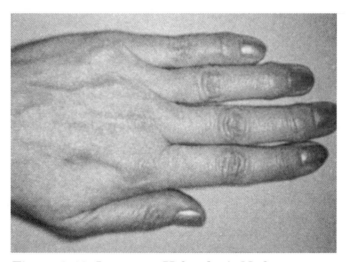

Figure 2-10. Lumps or Heberden's Nodes

Often, the swelling and pain have a tendency to disappear after a year or so, even though X-rays may show that the arthritis is getting progressively worse.

In the last two decades, surgical techniques have been developed for hip osteoarthritis. The procedure, replacement arthroplasty, involves total hip replacement by an orthopedic surgeon. Technically, the top of the thigh bone (known as "the head of the femur") is replaced with a steel ball on a stem. The cup of the pelvis (known as "the acetabulum") is replaced with a high density polyethylene cup. Both of the implants are secured to the living, normal bone with a fast-harden-

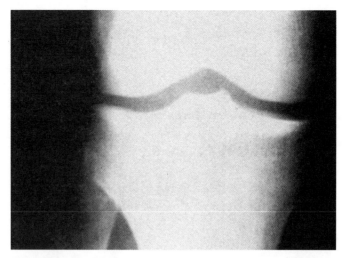

Figure 2-11. X-Ray of normal knee

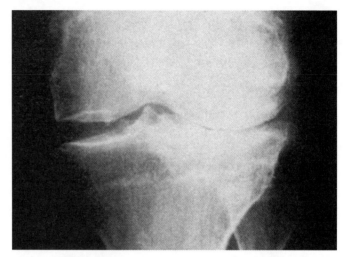

Figure 2-12. X-ray of Osteoarthritic knee

ing methylmethacrylate glue-like substance (Figure 2-13). Results are very impressive. However, because the operation is relatively new, it is impossible to predict the long term results. Similar operations have now been developed for the knees.

In Western medicine, the measures of relief from discomfort are usually provided by physicians. Treatment during the painful period may involve a variety of non-steroidal drugs or aspirin; rest and special muscle-strengthening exercises are recommended. Sometimes, an orthopedic specialist may be needed to decide if a condition of severe osteoarthritis requires special braces, exercises, or even surgical intervention.

## 4. Rheumatoid Arthritis:

Rheumatoid arthritis is a chronic inflammatory disease whose cause is still not clear (Figure 2-14), but may relate to disorders of the microcirculation of blood in the joint itself. Rheumatoid arthritis

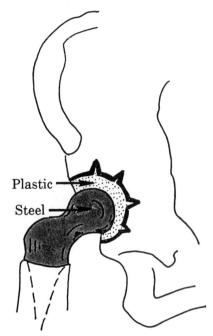

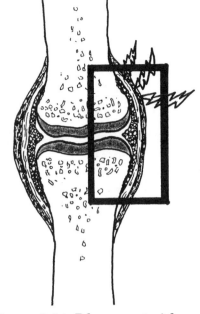

Figure 2-13. Hip joint replacement for osteoarthritis

Figure 2-14. Rheumatoid arthritis

affects people of all ages, and it may first appear in six-month-old babies or 60 year-old adults. The mean age of onset is around 30 to 40. Rheumatoid arthritis usually affects up to 15 or more joints at the same time, although in one form of the disease called "monoarticular rheumatoid arthritis" only one joint is affected.

The major problems for the patient with rheumatoid arthritis are joint destruction and pain. Different from many other forms of arthritis, rheumatoid arthritis has alternating periods of remission, when the symptoms disappear, and exacerbation, marked by the return of stiffness and pain. Typically, the disease can be active for months or years, then abate, sometimes permanently. It is still not known what causes the remission, though it is not believed to result from treatment.

Many tissues may be involved in the rheumatoid process, including the lungs, spleen, skin, and occasionally the heart. However, the primary target of rheumatoid arthritis is the synovium, the joint lining. This tissue, which should be smooth and velvety, becomes inflamed, rough, granulated, and swollen. Under the microscope, cells such as lymphocytes, plasma cells, and macrophages, all elements of the body's immune or disease-fighting apparatus, are visible in samples of the tissue. It is uncertain why they are there. The unusual presence of these cells is one of a series of clues that have led to a theory that rheumatoid arthritis may be a virus-initiated disease. It has been postulated that the synovial tissue contains an antigen, a substance which is capable of stimulating an immune reaction by which body tissues attempt to reject the

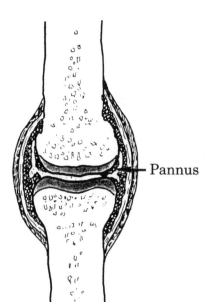

Pannus

Figure 2-15. Growth of pannus in
rheumatoid arthritis

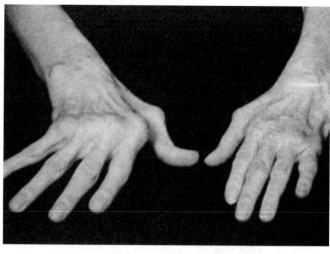

Figure 2-16. Deformities caused by rheumatoid
arthritis

antigenic material by attacking the joint. In this case, scientists think that one antigen present may be a virus. Although a virus may trigger or start this immune reaction, it is the effort of the body to reject the virus or antigen that causes pain and swelling and results in synovial destruction.

The immunological reaction that characterizes rheumatoid arthritis appears to stimulate a second reaction within connective tissue. Connective tissue forms the supporting structure of the body. It connects and surrounds the different organs and body parts and holds them in place. After a surgical incision, healing occurs by the proliferation of connective tissue. The result is a scar. Connective tissue contains the same kind of protein-collagen-which forms much of the structure of bone and cartilage. Tissue on both sides of the wound is restructured as fresh, new collagen is deposited there.

In rheumatoid arthritis, proliferating connective or granulation tissue invades the joint cartilage. Pannus or aprons of granulation tissue grow between and across the cartilages on both bones in the joint (Figure 2-15). It can also invade and destroy bone and ligaments.

The patient usually has swelling and pain in joints on both sides of the body, in a relatively symmetrical fashion. Stiffness is a major complaint, and as the disease progresses, deformities may appear. Even with very severe deformities, the joints can remain astonishingly flexible, and they are often not as painful as the deformities would suggest (Figure 2-16).

## 5. Juvenile Rheumatoid Arthritis:

Although rheumatoid arthritis is most common in adults, it does affect an estimated 200,000 American youngsters. Like adult arthritis, Juvenile Rheumatoid Arthritis (JRA) can sometimes begin with the swelling of many joints, although it can also begin with pain and swelling in a few joints or even a single joint. Commonly these symptoms may mistakenly be attributed to a fall or some other injury. Sometimes, before obvious signs of arthritis appear weeks or months later, JRA begins with a spiking fever, fleeting nonitching rash, and occasionally abdominal pain.

JRA is a difficult disease, but with early diagnosis and effective treatment, a relatively normal childhood can be preserved for most youngsters. Excellent functional status can eventually be regained in at least 80% of the patients, and remission (or disappearance of the disease) can occur in about two thirds of the cases. The optimal treatment for JRA, like adult rheumatoid arthritis, begins with aspirin. If aspirin is not adequate, gold salts or antimalarial drugs may be employed.

An exercise program tailored to the child's needs is at least as important as medication in maintaining joint function and muscle strength. For this, help from an expert physical therapist is needed. Most parents, with instruction from a therapist, become very competent cotherapists. Usually, a physician specializing in JRA is needed.

## 6. Ankylosing Spondylitis:

Ankylosing spondylitis (AS), also referred to as "poker spine," is a special form of arthritis which affects the small joints of the spine. It affects males more often than females. Diagnosis is usually made during young adulthood. The disorder is characterized by back pain, stiffness, and loss of spinal mobility due to the involvement of spinal joints. Later these joints tend to become fused and rigid. The stiffening may sometimes extend to the ribs, limiting the flexibility of the rib cage, so that breathing is impaired. The hips and shoulders may also become inflamed and stiff.

Though AS is not fatal, it is a serious disease, and if it is not treated it can result in permanently deformed posture. In its initial stages, AS can easily be confused with many other causes of back pain. For this reason, those afflicted with the disease are frequently misdiagnosed.

The disease is usually treated with pain-relieving and anti-inflammatory drugs. The drugs may sometimes produce side effects which can be eliminated when they are withdrawn. A recent study also indicates that aspirin may be effective for some patients and should be given a trial before resorting to the other drugs. Exercise, posture training, and orthopedic correction are also important aspects of the therapy. Practice of appropriate exercises and development of constructive habits of body use in everyday activities are very helpful as AS progresses. For this reason, early recognition of the disease is important.

### 7. Lyme Disease:

This disease is caused by a tick-borne spirochete (a form of bacteria). It is now clear that Lyme disease involves many parts of the body, including the skin, the joints, the heart, and the nervous system.

The joint lesions of Lyme disease are very similar to those of rheumatoid arthritis. A recently completed study suggests that the arthritis often seen in chronic Lyme disease may have an immuno-genetic basis (hereditary traits or genes that influence the immune response of the body.) Although 80 percent of patients may experience joint pain sometime during the course of the disease, only 10 percent develop chronic arthritis.

### 8. Lupus:

Systemic lupus erythematosus (SLE, or lupus) is a disorder of the body's immune system. It involves inflammation of the connective tissue, and can include arthritis when it affects the joints. The exact cause of lupus is unknown, but evidence suggests that it may result from a disorder in the body's production of antibodies (proteins that fight invading organisms).(*3) In lupus, the body produces abnormal antibodies or autoantibodies that react against the patient's own tissues. Virtually every organ system can be affected, including the central nervous system. Symptoms may include psychosis, convulsions, and myelitis (inflammation of the spinal cord). A recent study has shown that normal, healthy women who have recurrent miscarriages may also have an underlying connective tissue disease such as lupus.

### 9. Sjogren's Syndrome:

Sjogren's syndrome and systemic lupus erythrmatosus are two autoimmune connective tissue diseases with distinctive, but often overlapping clinical features.(*3) Sjogren's syndrome is marked by dryness of the eyes and mouth, caused by the destruction of the glands that secrete tears and saliva. It may be a primary disease, or it may be secondary to certain rheumatic diseases, such as rheumatoid arthritis, scleroderma or systemic lupus erythematosus.

### 10. Scleroderma:

Scleroderma, which literally means hard skin and is also known as progressive systemic sclerosis (PSS), is a connective tissue disorder in which excessive amounts of the protein collagen accumulate in the skin.(*3) It is a disease of the vascular (blood vessel) and immune systems, as well as a connective tissue disorder. The disease can affect internal organs such as the kidneys, lungs, heart, or gastrointestinal tract and cause them to thicken and harden, which seriously affects their functioning.

### 11. Reiter's Syndrome:

Reiter's syndrome is understood as a combination of urethritis, conjunctivitis, and arthritis.(*4) This arthritis affects the spine and peripheral joints and occurs most commonly in young male adults. Usually, the first attack lasts only a few weeks or months.

Although Reiter's syndrome is not considered a venereal disease, it appears to result from infection. For example, the sexual exposure to an infectious agent can often be the cause of this disease. In addition, the disease also appears after diarrhea, sometimes during epidemics. Research has shown that most patients with the disease have a genetic predisposition to it.

### 12. Fibromyalgia:

Fibromyalgia or fibrositis is a noninflammatory form of arthritis. It is characterized by aching and stiffness in joint and muscle areas that cannot yet be explained. Very often, the patient is tense, and usually has difficulty sleeping. Attacks may result from an injury, repeated muscular strain, prolonged mental tension, or depression. Fibromyalgia is not a destructive, progressive disease, nor is it disabling or crippling. However, it can be a debilitating problem for the patient and the misery can continue for years.

The condition of fibromyalgia may disappear spontaneously or as a result of treatment. Although a drug known as amitriptyline (an antidepressant) has proven helpful in reducing pain, sleep difficulty, fatigue, and joint tenderness, the most effective therapy has been teaching the person to relax, let go of neuromuscular tension, and to develop better habits of exercise and body use.

### 13. Polymyalgia Rheumatica:

Polymyalgia rheumatica usually afflicts people over the age of 50; it causes stiffness and severe aching in the shoulders and hips. Sometimes other joints ache as well, and a few may be swollen. If the disorder is not diagnosed and treated early, symptoms such as fever, fatigue, weight loss, and inflammation of the arteries may worsen. On rare occasions, the blood supply to the eye is affected, resulting in blindness.

The cause of polymyalgia is unknown. Without treatment, the disease may last for three years or more and can involve considerable pain and disability. Fortunately, the condition is dramatically relieved almost immediately with corticosteroid treatment. Prednisone is generally given and most patients are well within days and can resume normal activities. The drug does not cure the disease, but it eliminates the symptoms. Long-term treatment is usually necessary. The disease tends to disappear after a period of months or years.

### 2-4. Causes of Arthritis

Although we understand how some forms of arthritis start, we are still in the dark about other forms. In this section we would like to summarize the known possible causes, and also contribute some ideas from Chinese medicine and Qigong.

### 1. Weakness of the Internal Organs:

We already know that the condition of the internal organs is closely related to our health. According to Chinese medicine, there are five Yin organs which are considered the most important for our health and longevity. These organs are the heart, liver, lungs, kidneys, and spleen. Whenever any of these five organs is not functioning properly, sickness or even death can occur. Furthermore, all of these five organs are mutually interrelated. Whenever there is a problem with one, the others are always involved too. For example, gouty arthritis is caused by the improper functioning of the liver and kidneys.

## 2. Defective Genes:

Only recently it was reported that some forms of arthritis are caused by defective genes, which are inherited from one's parents. According to Chinese medicine, the genes are considered the essence of your being. This essence is responsible for the production of hormones, from which Qi is generated. When this Qi is led to the brain, the spirit is raised. When all of these conversion processes are functioning normally, the immune system is strong and sickness is less likely. One of the main goals of Qigong is learning how to convert the essence into Qi efficiently and lead it to the brain.

## 3. Weak Joints:

Weak joints can come from heredity or from lack of exercise. The body is a living machine, so the more you use it, the better condition it will be in. Chinese medicine believes that even if you have inherited a weak joint it is still possible to strengthen it through Qigong. When you exercise, Qi is brought to the joint by the movement of the muscles and tendons. This will nourish the joint and rebuild it.

## 4. Injury:

According to today's medicine, some forms of arthritis are caused by injury to the joints. Although the injury may not be serious, it may have significant results. The injury can affect the muscles, tendons, ligaments, or even the cartilage and bone. Whenever any joint injury, even a minor one, is not treated, the normal smooth Qi circulation in the joint area will be affected. If the situation persists, the Qi imbalance can cause problems such as arthritis.

## 5. Aging:

Aging has always been the cause of many sicknesses, including arthritis. When you are old, the Qi level in your body is low. Since your system is being deprived of the required amount of Qi, it starts to degenerate. One of the main goals of Qigong practice is learning how to slow down the aging process by building up the Qi in the body.

## 6. Qi Deficiency:

Qi deficiency is responsible for many problems. It can be caused by emotional depression and sadness, which can lead the Qi inward and make the body Yin. This deprives the outer body of Qi. When this happens, you will generally feel cold. If the problem persists for a long time, the muscles and tendons will be affected by the the lack of Qi, and the joints will be weakened.

Qi deficiency can have other causes, such as the weather. For example, your body's Qi is more deficient in the winter, and therefore, arthritis can be more serious then.

Qi deficiency can also be caused by working for prolonged periods in a damp area, or by exposing your joints to the cold.

### 7. Tension:
Tension includes both mental tension and physical tension, which are related and cannot be separated. Constant mental and physical tension can increase the pressure on the joints. For example, some people are very tense and grind their teeth in their sleep, which can cause arthritis in the jaw.

A lot of body tension is caused by the emotional disturbance which is related to your mental reaction to stressful events. For this reason, learning how to regulate your mind is an important part of the treatment of arthritis.

## 2-5. Other Possible Means of Preventing or Curing Arthritis
In addition to the ones already discussed, there are a number of other methods of preventing or curing arthritis. Although many of them are still awaiting scientific confirmation, they may be worth your consideration. However, you must understand that everybody has his or her own unique characteristics, and his or her own unique inheritance. In addition to the habits and lifestyle that each person has developed, everyone's mental and physical structure is different. For example, some people are affected by allergies while others are not. What this means is that you cannot necessarily use the same method to treat different people, even when they have the same disease. Even modern Western medicine has found that the same treatment will not work equally well on all patients. Therefore, do not automatically brush off some of the treatment methods we will discuss. After all, Western medicine is only in its infancy, and it may come to understand and accept these alternative remedies.

### 1. Diet:
People who are experienced in Qigong have always considered food to be a significant influence on the condition of the Qi in the body. For this reason, diet is one of the main concerns of Chinese medicine. There is a saying: "You are what you eat." It is well known that improper diet is one of the main causes of gouty arthritis. The Chinese have found many different herbs that can ease the pain and reduce the swelling of arthritis. It has recently been discovered that protein, calories, and fats can reduce the inflammation of arthritis. Certain fish oils may interfere with the process of inflammation and therefore reduce the symptoms of rheumatoid arthritis.(*5, *6).

### 2. Change of Residence:
Since the Qi in your environment can affect the Qi in your body, arthritis sufferers should give serious consideration to this method. If the climate where you live is too damp or too cold, it may be affecting your arthritis. It has recently been discovered that the Qi in our bodies can be significantly affected by the electromagnetic fields gen-

erated by modern technology, and therefore cause some forms of cancer. For example, people who live near high tension power lines tend to get cancer more often than those who do not. Perhaps similar environmental effects on arthritis will be found.

### 3. Change of Lifestyle:

Your lifestyle affects how the Qi circulates in your body. If you frequently feel ill, especially mentally, you might need to change your lifestyle. How you think and how you coordinate the Qi pattern in your body with the natural Qi is very important for your health. Whenever your Qi circulation is against the "Dao" (nature), you will be sick. You may find that walking for an hour or doing Qigong exercises every morning improves your Qi circulation.

### 4. Clothing:

What you wear also affects the Qi in your body. In the winter you must stay warm, and especially protect your joints. Joints that are left unprotected can loose Qi very quickly.

It has been discovered that many man-made fibers can adversely affect the Qi distribution and circulation in the body. For example, polyester is known to cause Qi stagnation, and to prevent the body's Qi from exchanging with the environmental Qi. You may have noticed that clothing made of polyester can accumulate a considerable charge of static electricity in the winter. This builds up an electromagnetic field and affects the Qi circulation in your body.

There are many other ways of improving the condition of your arthritis. For example, it is reported that sexual activity can stimulate the adrenal glands to produce more corticosteroid, a hormone that reduces joint inflammation and pain. It is believed that sexual activity may also trigger the release of endorphins, a naturally-occurring painkilling substance.(*7)

You can see from our brief discussion that, if we want to understand arthritis completely, we must remain humble and continue our study and research. Only then will we be able to reach the goal of a complete cure.

# References

(*1). "Medicine for the Layman - Arthritis," Clinical Center Office of Clinical Reports & Inquiries, Building 10B, Room 1C255, Bethesda, Maryland, 20892.

(*2). "The Complete Medical Guide," Benjamin F. Miller, M.D., Simon and Schuster, New York, 1978.

(*3). "Arthritis, Rheumatic Diseases, and Related Disorders," U.S. Department of Health and Human Services, Public Health Service, National Institutes of Health.

(*4). "An Overview of Arthritis and Related Disorders," Caring, January 1989.

(*5). "Arthritis and Diet," Arthritis Foundation, 1314 Spring Street, N.W., Atlanta, GA 30309.

(*6). "Can Diet Relieve Arthritis," University of California, Berkeley, Wellness Letter, Volume 6, Issue 8.

(*7). "Arthritis and Your Love Life," 8, Men's Health, 1989.

# Chapter 3
# How do the Chinese Treat Arthritis?

In the first chapter we said that the actual definition of "Qigong" is "the study of Qi." This means that Qigong actually covers a very wide field of research, and includes the study of the three general types of Qi (Heaven Qi, Earth Qi, and Human Qi) and their interrelationships. However, because the Chinese have traditionally paid more attention to the study of Human Qi, which is concerned with health and longevity, the term "Qigong" has often been misunderstood and misused to mean only the study of Human Qi. Because so much attention has been given to Human Qi over thousands of years, human Qigong has reached a very high level. Today it includes many fields such as acupuncture, herbal study, massage, cavity press, Qigong exercises, and even martial arts.

In this chapter I would like to summarize, according to my understanding, some of the methods commonly used in China to prevent arthritis, to ease its pain, and to cure it. I would then like to focus the discussion on how Qigong uses massage (including cavity press) and exercises to prevent and cure arthritis. Finally, I would like to point out the differences in how Western and Chinese medicine use massage and exercise to treat arthritis.

## 3-1. General Chinese Treatments for Arthritis
The best way to treat arthritis is to prevent it from happening. However, if it has already occurred, then the appropriate course is to prevent it from getting any worse, and then to rebuild the strength of the joint so that it can resume functioning normally.

Generally speaking, if a case of arthritis has already reached the stage of serious physical damage, special treatment is needed before any rebuilding can proceed. During the treating and rebuilding process, alleviating pain is always the first concern. In this section we will briefly discuss the theory of several common methods for treating arthritis which have been developed in China.

## 1. Massage:

When done properly, massage will improve the Qi circulation in the joint area. Massage is commonly used when a patient suffers from Feng Shi, before arthritis and physical damage have occurred. At this time the Qi circulation is unbalanced, which may affect the nerves around the joints and cause pain. As mentioned earlier, Feng Shi can occur when a joint is weak or injured, or when a joint has degenerated because of aging. The pain usually increases when rain is coming on, because clouds and moisture accumulate great masses of electric charges which affect the Qi in our bodies. Pain can also occur when the joints are exposed to cold wind, which can significantly affect the Qi of the joints.

If the Feng Shi is caused by a minor injury, massage can help to heal the injury and ease the pain. This can usually prevent the Feng Shi from developing into arthritis, which the Chinese call "joint infection" (Guan Jie Yan). However, if the Feng Shi is caused by a weak joint or one degenerated because of aging, then once the pain is alleviated, Qigong exercises are necessary to rebuild the strength of the joint and prevent the Feng Shi from returning and developing into arthritis.

Massage is not used just to heal Feng Shi. It is very effective in increasing Qi circulation and easing the pain even when the joint infection (arthritis) has already become serious. However, because massage cannot reach deep enough into the body, it is not wise to rely on it for a cure.

## 2. Acupuncture:

Acupuncture is another method of temporarily stopping the pain and increasing the Qi circulation in the joint area to help the healing. The main difference between massage and acupuncture is that the former usually stays only on the surface, while the latter can reach to the center of the joint. One of the advantages of acupuncture is that, if the arthritis is caused by an old injury deep in the joint, it can heal the injury or at least remove some of the stagnated Qi or bruise.

In acupuncture, needles or other newly developed means such as lasers or electricity are used to stimulate and increase the Qi circulation. Although acupuncture can stop the pain and can, to some degree, cure the arthritis, the process can be so time-consuming as to be emotionally draining. Acupuncture is an external method, and while it may remove the symptoms, it can usually heal arthritis only temporarily or only to a limited degree. Rebuilding the strength of the joint is a long term proposition. Therefore, after arthritis patients have received some treatment, the physician will frequently encourage them to get involved in Qigong exercises to rebuild the joint.

### 3.  Herbal Treatments:

Herbal treatments are used together with massage and acupuncture, especially when the arthritis is caused by an injury. The herbs are usually made into a paste or ground into powder, mixed with a liquid such as alcohol, and then applied to the joint. The dressing is changed every twenty-four hours.

Herbal treatments are used to alleviate pain, to increase the Qi circulation and help the healing of the injury, and to speed up the process of regrowth. Patients who are rebuilding weak joints through Qigong exercises can speed the process with herbal treatments.

### 4.  Cavity Press:

Cavity Press (Dian Xue) is the method of using the fingertips (especially the thumb tip) to press acupuncture cavities and certain other points (pressure points) on the body in order to manipulate the Qi circulation. Acupuncture cavities are tiny spots distributed over the entire body where the Qi of the body can be manipulated through massage or the insertion of needles. According to the new theory of bioelectricity, these cavities are places where the electrical conductivity is higher than in neighboring areas. They are therefore more sensitive to external stimulation, and allow it to reach to the primary Qi channels.(*1)  Strictly speaking, cavity press (acupressure) should be discussed under massage. However, its theory is deeper and somewhat different from general massage. General massage covers a larger area of the joint, while cavity press focuses on the acupuncture cavities and certain non-acupuncture points. Normally, the power in cavity press can reach much deeper than in general massage. Furthermore, cavity press mostly uses the Qi channels to improve Qi circulation inside the joint, while general massage can enhance Qi circulation only superficially.

The theory of cavity press is very similar to that of acupuncture. There are a few differences, however: a. acupuncture uses needles or other means of penetration such as lasers, while cavity press uses the fingertips to press the cavities; b. acupuncture can reach much deeper than cavity press; c. cavity press is easier and more convenient than acupuncture, which requires equipment and a higher level of training. This means that anyone can learn to use cavity press to treat arthritis after only a short period of training and some experience. However, it takes years of study to learn acupuncture; d. a patient can use cavity press on him or herself much more easily than acupuncture.

In cavity press, stagnant Qi deep in the joint is led to the surface. This improves the Qi circulation in the joint area, and considerably reduces the pain. The use of cavity press to speed up the healing of injured joints is very common in the Chinese martial arts.

### 5.  Qigong Exercises:

The main purpose of Qigong exercises for arthritis is to rebuild the strength of the joint by improving the Qi circulation. As mentioned earlier, traditional Chinese physicians believe that since the body's cells are alive, as long as there is a proper supply of Qi the physical damage can be repaired or even completely rebuilt. They have proven that broken bones can be mended completely, even in the elderly. Even some Western physicians have now come to believe that damaged or degenerated joints can be returned to their original healthy state.(*2)

Practicing Qigong can not only heal arthritis or joint injury and rebuild the joint, it is also known to be very effective in strengthening the internal organs. Many illnesses, including some forms of arthritis, stem from abnormally functioning internal organs. For example, gouty arthritis is caused by an improperly functioning liver and kidneys.(*3)

According to Chinese medicine, almost all illnesses are caused by abnormal Qi circulation. Internal organs are the machines which produce and manage the circulation of Qi. Keeping them healthy is the key to health and longevity, and Qigong is one of the most effective ways of doing this. Chinese physicians also believe that when the internal organs are healthy, the immune system will be healthy and the potential for resisting sickness will be high. A weak immune system is responsible for many illnesses, and is considered to be closely related to the occurrence of arthritis. For examples lupus erythematosus, rheumatoid arthritis, lyme disease, sjogren's syndrome, and scleroderma are all linked to a weak immune system.(*3, *4)

Before we discuss massage and exercise Qigong, let us first summarize the differences in how Chinese and Western medicine treat arthritis.

**Summary:**
**1. Prevention:**
**Western medicine:**
There are few documents which discuss how to prevent arthritis. It just does not seem to be considered important. When the symptoms of arthritis appear, treatment is started. Even if there is some joint pain, if there is no sign of arthritis in the X-rays the physician may prescribe some medication for the pain, but other than that, he or she will all too often tend to ignore it.

**Chinese medicine:**
When a patient has a joint injury, Chinese physicians will first usually use acupuncture, massage, and herbal treatment to eliminate any bruises or Qi stagnation inside the joint. When the injury is almost healed, the physician will encourage the patient to do Qigong exercises to increase the Qi circulation and speed the healing. The most important effect of the Qigong, however, is to insure that all the bruises and stagnation in the joint are cleared up. This can be done only through the patient moving the joint. If this is

not done, the bruises and stagnation will eventually develop into Feng Shi and continue to interfere with smooth and balanced Qi circulation in the joint.

In China, when people start getting older and feel their bodies getting weaker, they will often start practicing some form of Qigong such as Taijiquan (*5) or Ba Duan Jin (The Eight Pieces of Brocade)(*6). This helps them to keep their Qi circulating smoothly and to slow down the degeneration of their bodies. It also prevents Feng Shi and arthritis. Most people find that, in addition to strengthening their limbs, they are also able to restore their internal organs to full health, which is the key to health and longevity.

## 2. Stopping the Pain:
### Western medicine:

Western medicine sometimes uses massage to alleviate pain, but more commonly drugs such as aspirin, prednisone, naprosyn, motrin, colchicine, and many others are prescribed. The problem with drugs is that very often they have side effects, such as the dis-- turbance of the gastrointestinal tract and skin rash caused by using motrin, and the weakening or damaging of the internal organs caused by other medicines.(*1) This is a very common problem in Western medicine, which will frequently cure one problem only to inflict another one on the patient.

### Chinese medicine:

Acupuncture, massage, cavity press, and herbal treatments are commonly used to stop the pain. This is only to make the patient feel more comfortable, and is not considered part of the healing.

## 3. Healing:
### Western medicine:

Drugs can be effective in treating some forms of arthritis. For example, certain drugs can be used to regulate the liver and the kidneys, curing gouty arthritis. This can get quick results. However, the patient is then tied to the drugs, which may eventually disturb the normal functioning of some organs.

When the arthritis has become serious, the joint can now be replaced with an artificial one. However, the long term effect of these replacement joints is still unknown.(*3, *4)

Doctors now encourage arthritis patients to do certain exercises, often with significant results. However, documentation and more experimentation are still needed. For example, are there some forms of exercise which are harmful rather than beneficial to arthritis patients? So far, there is no established authority on this subject.

Electricity is now being used to speed up the healing of broken bones. As the West increases its understanding of bioelectricity (Qi), it is quite possible that ways will be found to use electricity to speed the healing and regrowth of arthritic joints.

**Chinese medicine:**

Massage, cavity press, and/or acupuncture are usually used first to increase the Qi circulation. If the arthritis is not too serious, this may be sufficient for a cure. However, if the condition has become serious, external and internal herbal treatments are also called for. The herbs taken internally are to increase the Qi circulation, remove bruises, or prevent further infection of the joint. Chinese medicine seeks to cure the cause of the arthritis. For example, if it is caused by an injury, then bruises and Qi stagnation must be cleared up. And if the arthritis is caused by degeneration due to aging, then Qigong exercises must be used to rebuild the joint and slow the degeneration.

In the next section we will discuss in more detail how massage and exercise Qigong can prevent and cure arthritis.

### 3-2. How Can Qigong Cure Arthritis?

In Chinese medicine, the concept of Qi is used both in the diagnosis and in the treatment. A basic principle of Chinese medicine is that you have to rebalance the Qi before you can cure the root of a disease. Only then can you also repair the physical damage and rebuild your physical strength and health. The theory is very simple. Your entire body is made up of living cells. When these cells receive the proper Qi supply, they will function normally and even repair themselves. However, if the Qi supply is abnormal, and this condition persists, then even though the cells were originally healthy, they will be damaged or changed (perhaps even becoming cancerous). In light of this basic Qi theory, let us first discuss why Qigong can be effective in curing arthritis. Then we will explain how Chinese massage and Qigong work, and finally we will point out the main differences in how Western and Chinese medicine use massage and exercise to treat arthritis.

**Why Qigong is Effective for Arthritis:**
**1. Qigong Maintains and Increases Smooth Qi Circulation.**

As mentioned earlier, the goal of Qigong healing is to reestablish a strong, smooth flow of Qi through the affected area. When this happens, the physical damage can be repaired and the strength rebuilt. Chinese physicians have always believed that as long as you are alive, physical damage to the body can be repaired through improving the Qi and blood circulation. Most Western physicians don't agree with this, and believe, for example, that the osteoarthritis caused by aging and the degeneration of the joints cannot be reversed. However, some Western physicians are beginning to change their minds about this.(*2)

**2. Qigong Strengthens the Organs.**

The greatest benefit of Chinese Qigong is probably in the training that is designed to regulate the Qi circulating in the internal organs. We know that these organs are vital, and if there is any problem with them we can become sick or even die. Regulating their Qi and keeping them healthy is a major goal of Qigong. In the more advanced Qigong practices the training goes even deeper, and is concerned with strengthening and improving the health of the organs. These practices balance the Yin and Yang Qi in the organs to slow down the aging process. Since the internal organs manage the various functions of your body, you have to take care of them first if you want to slow down the aging process.

The Qi circulating in your body is the source of your life. When this circulation stops, you die. Let us look again at the source or origin of your Qi. Qi is energy, and it has to be produced from matter. As explained in the first chapter, the Chinese believe that the body contains two types of material which can be converted into Qi: one is called Pre-birth essence, and the other Post-birth essence. The Pre-birth essence is inherited from your parents, while the Post-birth essence is in the food and the air which you take in after your birth. Only in this century was it discovered that Pre-birth essence is actually the hormones produced by the endocrine glands. Since the quality and quantity of the hormones you produce depends on the inherent strength of your body, which was determined by the genes you received from your parents, Qigong practitioners used to believe that the genes were the Pre-birth essence.

The formation of your organs is controlled by your genes. Once you are born your organs are significantly affected by your lifestyle, which includes your thinking (emotional disturbances), food, air, and even the weather that you are exposed to. Your internal organs convert food and air into the Qi which circulates in your body. Any trouble in the internal organs will affect the production of Qi. Remember: Only when your internal organs are healthy will you have a normal supply of Qi, and only then will you be able to manage your life efficiently.

Your Qi can be affected by defects in your organs. The physical body is closely related to the Qi, and they affect each other. Whenever the Qi loses balance, its manifestation in the physical body will be abnormal. We know today that many diseases not confined to the organs are caused by the abnormal functioning of the organs. You can see that the condition of the internal organs is actually the foundation of your health and longevity.

### 3. Qigong Strengthens the Immune and Hormone Production Systems.

Western science knows that the body's immune system is closely related to the endocrine glands, which produce hormones. Hormones, as they are now understood, do not actually create processes. What they do, however, is cause the fundamental processes such as growth and reproduction to speed up or slow down. (The word hormone comes from the Greek word *hormōn*, which means to excite, to stimulate, or to stir up.) They also strengthen the ability of the immune system to fight diseases. For example, it is believed that the thymus gland (which is located just behind the top of the sternum) plays an important role in the body's immune system. Exactly how this happens is still not completely understood. We still do not know very much about the pineal gland in the upper back part of the brain, nor do we have a full understanding of the function of the thymus.(*7) In fact, it has only recently come to be believed that hormone production is significantly related to the aging process.

Many of us know of people who were deathly sick, but who had a very high spirit and a strong desire to survive, and miraculously recovered. Both Western and Eastern religions tell of many such cases. Chinese Qigong practitioners believe that if a sick person can lead Qi to the brain through concentration or through a strong desire, he or she can evoke a powerful healing force. A possible explanation is that the stronger Qi flow activates the pineal and pituitary glands so that they generate more hormones. We now know that the most important function of the pituitary gland is to stimulate, regulate, and coordinate the functions of the other endocrine glands.(*7) For this reason it is sometimes called the "master gland."

In Chinese Qigong, the Upper Dan Tian (which some Westerners refer to as the "third eye") is considered the center of your whole being. If you raise your spirit, which resides there, you can energize your body, generate amazing physical and mental strength, and recover more quickly from injury or sickness. Certain groups in the West have also recognized its importance as the center of the spirit, and consider it a "third eye" which is able to sense further than the physical eyes can see.

If we combine the understanding of old and new, East and West, we can conclude that what actually happens, probably because of mental concentration, is that a stronger current of bioelectricity is led to the pineal and pituitary glands to activate the production of hormones. This stimulates the entire endocrine system and causes it to function more effectively, improving healing, reproduction, and growth. If this is correct, then it is possible to begin a new era of scientific self-healing or spiritual healing. An alternative result is that we may learn how to devise electrical equipment to activate the pineal and pituitary glands to improve the effectiveness and speed of healing. Perhaps we may also be able to find the secret key to slowing down the aging process.

### 4. Qigong Raises the Spirit of Vitality.

The spirit is closely tied to the mind, and cannot be separated from it. In Qigong practice, the mind is considered the general in the battle against sickness. When the mind (general) has a strong will, thoroughly understands the battlefield (the body), wisely and carefully sets up the strategy (the breathing technique), and effectively and efficiently manages the soldiers (the Qi), then the morale (spirit) of the general and soldiers can be high. When this happens, sickness can be conquered and health regained.

When you use Qigong to treat your arthritis, you must first treat your mind by changing the way you look at your sickness and your life. The first thing you need to do is to stop passively accepting the negative things that have happened to you. Become more active and take charge of your life. Most basically, learn how to keep the pain of arthritis from disturbing your peace of mind. Remember, doing something is better than doing nothing.

Second, you must rebuild your confidence in your ability to treat your arthritis. Even though you may have failed before, don't let that discourage you. Learn about the causes of your problem, understand the theory of this new treatment, and try to think about how you can make the treatment more effective. Once you have done this, you will have rebuilt your confidence not only in the treatment, but also in your life.

Once you have built up your confidence, the third thing you need to do is to develop the willpower, patience, and perseverance needed to keep up the treatment. The best way to prevent the arthritis from returning once you have cured it is to make Qigong part of your life.

Fourth, after you have practiced Qigong for a while, you will understand your body better and you will know how to deal with the problems more easily. You may realize that the pain is not necessarily all bad. Pain draws your attention to your body and helps you to understand yourself better. Pain can also help you to build up willpower and perseverance. However, you must first know what pain is, only then will you know how to stop it. This is called "regulating your mind." Remember that medicine is only a temporary solution.

You can see that Chinese Qigong heals by going to the root of the problem. It improves the entire body, both mentally and physically, and strengthens the immune system. Only when this is done will the illness be healed completely. Now that you understand why Qigong can cure arthritis, let us discuss how Qigong reaches this goal.

### How Can Qigong Exercises Cure Arthritis and How Are They Different From Western Arthritis Exercises?

You probably already know that Western physicians recommend exercise for arthritis, and that many books and reports of experiments have been published.(*8-*13) Regardless of whether or not you are familiar with these exercises, you should first understand the differences between the exercises used by Chinese Qigong and the exercises which are recommended by Western arthritis physicians. Then your mind will be clear, and you will be able to practice effectively.

First let us review the basic theory of the arthritis exercises used in the West which have proven effective. Naturally, there is no doubt that many of these theories, and even some of the practices are consistent with those of Chinese Qigong.

According to the Western conception, the key to healing arthritis is that the patient must learn how to balance exercise and rest.

This means that without exercise there is no hope of healing, but too much exercise will worsen the arthritic condition. Therefore, since each individual has his or her own body and specific arthritic conditions, they must first understand their condition and then use common sense to regulate their lifestyle and exercise.

Western medicine believes that exercise has several benefits for the physical body: a. it increases the strength and flexibility of the muscles and ligaments surrounding the joints; b. it maintains or increases bone strength; c. some active types of exercises such as long distance walking and swimming have important effects on the heart that can promote increased endurance and circulation and fight deterioration of the arteries. It is believed that even a small amount of exercise will help the patient overcome fatigue.

The basic Western theory of how exercise is able to heal arthritis is very simple. Every tissue in your body requires nutrition to work normally and effectively, and most tissues have arteries to carry these requirements to them. However, the situation is quite different for the joint cartilage. In the joints, movement is the only way that nourishment can be brought by the synovial fluid to the cartilage and that waste products can be removed. This means that exercise promotes good joint nutrition.

According to their different purposes, there are three general types of exercise recommended by Western physicians. The first type is stretching. Usually this type of exercise is designed to maintain and improve joint mobility, and consequently it decreases pain and improves function. In this type of exercise, the joint is moved or stretched as far as it will comfortably go and then pushed a little further to just past the point where pain or discomfort begins.

The second type of exercise is to increase muscle strength and consequently lend stability to vulnerable joints. However, the exercises designed for this purpose should minimize stress on the joints to avoid further injury. Therefore, many of these exercises are designed to extend and contract the muscles without moving the joints. An example of this is squeezing the fists tight and then relaxing them.

When the joint has partially recovered, the third step is to insure that it stays healthy. This is accomplished through endurance exercises such as walking, swimming, bicycling, jogging, or dancing to promote cardiovascular fitness. An ideal arthritis exercise program should include all three types.

You can see from this review how Western arthritis exercises are able to treat arthritis. What, then, are the differences between it and Chinese Qigong?

1. From the theoretical point of view, Qigong originated from the concept of regulating the Qi (from an imbalanced condition into a balanced one) both before and after any physical damage has occurred. Western medicine, however, does not yet fully accept the existence of Qi or bioelectricity, and is therefore not concerned with it.

**2.** Chinese Qigong considers the regulation of the body to be the most basic and important factor in successful practice. Regulating the body means to bring your body into a very relaxed, centered, and balanced state. Only then can your mind be calm and comfortable. When the body is relaxed, the Qi can circulate freely and be led easily anywhere you wish, such as to the skin or even deep into the bone marrow and the internal organs. To cure arthritis, you have to be so relaxed that you can lead the Qi deep into the joint where it can repair the damage. Western arthritis exercises are not usually specifically concerned with relaxation.

The first priority in Qigong exercises for arthritis is learning how to relax and avoid muscle/tendon tension and stress in the joint area, which is especially critical in severe cases of arthritis. Chinese physicians reason that exercises which tense the muscles and tendons will inhibit the Qi circulation from going deep into the damaged joint. Furthermore, tension of the muscles and tendons increases pressure on the joint and can increase the damage. Therefore, Chinese physicians recommend relaxed, gentle movements first to smoothly increase the Qi circulation. Only when the patient has rebuilt the strength of the joint will the muscles and tendons be exercised. After all, strong muscles and tendons are what will prevent future joint damage.

**3.** With Qigong, in addition to the body being relaxed, the breathing must be long, deep, and calm. According to Qigong theory, breathing is the strategy of your practice. When you exhale you instinctively and naturally lead Qi to the surface of your body, and when you inhale you lead it inward to the bone marrow and the internal organs. In Qigong you have to learn to breathe deeply and calmly in coordination with your thinking. This way your mind can lead the Qi strongly into the damaged area. In Western arthritis exercises, only a few reports even mention breathing.(*8)

**4.** In the first chapter we explained that since the mind is one of the major forces (EMF) of Qi or bioelectric circulation, it has an important role in healing. In order to make your Qigong practice really effective, and in addition to regulating your body and breathing, you must also regulate your mind. Regulating your mind means to lead it away from outside distractions and turn it toward feeling what is going on inside your body. In order to lead Qi to the damaged places in your body, your mind must be calm, relaxed, and concentrated so that you can feel or sense the Qi. The mind, therefore, plays a very important role in Qigong. Western arthritis exercises, on the other hand, are usually not concerned at all with the mind.

**5.** Another significant difference between Qigong and Western arthritis exercises is that Qigong emphasizes not only healing the joints, but also rebuilding the health of the internal organs. Remember, only when the internal organs are healthy can the root of the Qi imbalance be removed and, therefore, the cause of the sickness be corrected. But Qigong is not just concerned with bringing the organs back to health, it also works to strengthen them. The Western arthritis exercises, in contrast, are not at all concerned with the health of the internal organs.

**6.** One of the most significant results of Qigong practice is maintaining hormone production at a healthy level, which keeps the immune system functioning effectively. In Western medicine, imbalanced hormone production is adjusted with drugs.

**7.** The most significant difference between Qigong and Western arthritis exercise is probably that practicing Qigong draws the patient gradually into an acquaintance with the inner energy of his or her body. Once this is experienced, patients can start to feel energy imbalances when they are just beginning, and consequently are able to correct them before physical damage occurs. In fact, this is the key to preventing most illnesses.

Although many of the movements of Qigong and Western arthritis exercises are similar, the theory of Qigong is more profound and therefore the challenge is more significant. In fact, the best way to maintain your health and rebuild your Qi and body is by understanding the theory of Qigong and starting the training.

Because this book will also introduce Qigong massage for arthritis, we would like to point out some of the major differences between Qigong massage and regular Western massage.

### How Chinese Qigong Massage Differs From Western Massage?

**1.** Chinese massage pays attention to improving the circulation of both Qi and blood, while Western massage normally emphasizes only good blood circulation and a comfortable, easy feeling.

**2.** In Chinese massage, the massager and the patient must communicate with each other both through touch and through deeper levels of contact. This mutual cooperation enables the massager to use his or her mind to either lead Qi into the patient or to remove excess Qi from the patient's body. Therefore, Qigong massage requires a higher level of experience and training in concentration. This means that the massage is not limited to only a physical massage, it is also a Qi massage. The most important part of this cooperation is that the patient can use his or her own mind to relax the area being massaged and make the massage more effective. Furthermore, this cooperation helps the patient to calm the mind and relax deeply into the internal organs and bone marrow, which makes it possible for the massage to regulate the Qi. In Western massage, the coordination between the massager and the patient is not emphasized.

**3.** Cavity press or acupressure techniques are considered part of Qigong massage. Like Japanese Shiatsu massage, which is derived from Chinese acupressure, finger pressure on the cavities is used to regulate the Qi circulation and to remove Qi and blood stagnation in the affected areas. To do this kind of massage effectively requires not only that the massager know the location of the cavities, but that he or she also understand the twelve Qi channels and how to use them to remove excess Qi from affected areas and bring in nourishing Qi. It is also extremely helpful if the massager is experienced in Qigong. This kind of practice is almost completely ignored in Western massage.

After reading this you may be discouraged about the possibility of your ever using Qigong massage techniques. As a matter of fact, you do not need such a high level of knowledge to deal with arthritis. All you really need to know is the location of the cavities or pressure points around the afflicted joint and how to apply pressure with your finger. With a bit of practice you will soon learn how to regulate the Qi there. After you have gained some experience you may even wish to study Qigong massage and learn more about using it for healing. In this book we will focus only on the massage and cavity press techniques which are related to arthritis. If you are interested in pursuing the subject in more depth, read the book "Qigong Massage" which will be published in the near future by YMAA.

# References

(*1). "The Body Electric," by Dr. Robert O. Becker, MD., and Gary Selden, 1985. William Marrow and Company, Inc., 105 Madison Ave., New York, 10016.

(*2). "Keeping the Human Body Active Reduces Risk of Osteoarthritis," by Dr. Gifford-Jones, Globe and Mail, Toronto, Ont., January 31, 1989.

(*3). "Medicine for the Layman - Arthritis," Clinical Center Office of Clinical Reports & Inquiries, Building 10B, Room 1C255, Bethesda, Maryland, 20892.

(*4). "An Overview of Arthritis and Related Disorders," Caring, January 1989.

(*5). "The Essence of Tai Chi Chi Kung," Dr. Yang Jwing-Ming, YMAA, 1990.

(*6). "The Eight Pieces of Brocade," Dr. Yang Jwing-Ming, YMAA, 1988.

(*7). "The Complete Medical Guide," Benjamin F. Miller, M.D., Simon and Schuster, New York, 1978.

(*8). "Use It or Lose It," Kate Lorig, R. N., Dr. P. H., and James F. Fries, M.D., Aim Plus, January/February, 1989.

(*9). "The Good News About Exercises," Peggy Person, Arthritis Today, May/June, 1989.

(*10). "How to Choose the Right Exercise," Arthritis Today, January/February, 1987.

(*11). "Understanding Arthritis," Irving Kushner, M.D., Charles Scribner's Sons, New York, 1984.

(*12). "Exercise and Arthritis," Richard S. Panush and David G. Brown, Sports Medicine 4: 54-64, 1987.

(*13). "Ostero-Arthritis," Fred L. Savage, Station Hill Press, Barrytown, New York, 1988.

# Chapter 4
# Qigong for Arthritis

## 4-1. Introduction

Before proceeding any further, we would first like to discuss the attitude which you need to adopt in your practice. Quite frequently, people who are ill are reluctant to get involved in the healing process. This is especially true for arthritis patients. Both Western and Chinese physicians have had difficulty persuading them to get involved in regular exercise or Qigong. The main reason for this reluctance is that the patients are afraid of pain, and therefore believe that these kinds of exercise are harmful. In order to conquer this obstacle to your healing, you must understand the theory of healing and the reason for practicing. Only then will you have the confidence necessary for continued practice. Remember, a physician may have an excellent prescription for your illness, but if you don't take the medicine, it won't do you any good.

Another factor which has caused the failure of many a potential cure is laziness. Because the healing process is very slow, it is very easy to become impatient and lazy. Very often in life we will know exactly what it is that we need to do, but because we are controlled by the emotional parts of our minds, we end up either not doing what we need to, or not doing it right. Either way, our efforts have all been in vain.

It seems that most of the time our "emotional mind" and "wisdom mind" are in opposition. In China there is a proverb which says: "You are your own biggest enemy." This means that your emotional mind often wants to go in the opposite direction from what your wisdom mind knows is best. If your wisdom mind is able to conquer your emotional mind, then there is nothing that can stop you from doing anything you want. Usually, however, your emotional mind makes you lazy, causes you to feel embarrassment (i.e., put a mask on your face), and destroys your willpower and perseverance. We always know that our clear-headed wisdom mind understands what needs to be done, but too often we surrender to our emotional mind and become slaves of our emotions. When this happens, we usually feel guilty deep down in our hearts, and we try to find a good excuse so that we won't have to feel so guilty.

The first step when you decide to practice Qigong is to strengthen your wisdom mind and use it to govern your emotional mind. Only then will you have enough patience and perseverance to keep practicing. You can see that the first key to successful training is not the techniques themselves but rather your self-control. I sincerely believe that as long as you have a strong will, patience, and perseverance, there is nothing that you can't accomplish.

Forming the habit of practicing regularly actually represents changing your lifestyle. Once you have started regulating your life through Qigong, it can not only cure your arthritis and restrengthen your joints, but it can also keep you healthy and make both your mental and physical lives much happier.

This chapter will focus on discussing the Qigong practices I am familiar with, leaving other methods, such as acupuncture and herbs to other references. Before we discuss the actual practices, we would first like to remind you of the keys to successful practice. Only if you follow these keys in your practice will you be able to see and feel how Chinese Qigong is different from similar Western arthritis exercises.

**Important Training Keys:**
**1.  Regulating the Body:**
Before you start your Qigong exercises, you should first calm down your mind and use this mind to bring your body into a calm and relaxed state. Naturally, you should always be concerned with your mental and physical centers. Only then will you be able to find your balance. When you have both mental and physical relaxation, centering, and balance, you will be both natural and comfortable. This is the key to regulating your body.

When you relax, you should learn to relax deeply into your internal organs, and especially the muscles which enclose the organs. In addition, you must also place your mind on the joints that are giving you trouble. The more you can bring your mind deep into the joint and relax it, the more Qi will circulate smoothly and freely to repair the damage.

**2.  Regulating the Breathing:**
As mentioned before, breathing is the central strategy in Qigong practice. According to Qigong theory, when you inhale you lead Qi inward and when you exhale you lead Qi outward. This is our natural instinct. For example, when you feel cold in the wintertime, in order to keep from loosing Qi out of your body you naturally inhale more than you exhale to lead the Qi inward, which also closes the pores in the skin. However, in the summertime when you are too hot you naturally exhale more than inhale in order to lead Qi out of your body. When you do this you start to sweat and the pores open.

In Qigong you want to lead the Qi to the internal organs and bone marrow, so you must learn how to use inhalation to lead the Qi inward. When you use Qigong to cure your arthritis, you must inhale and exhale deeply and calmly so that you can lead the Qi deep into the joint and also outward to dissipate the excess or stagnant Qi which has accumulated in the joints. Therefore, in addition to relaxing when you practice, you should always remember to inhale and exhale deeply. When you inhale, place your mind deep in the joint, and when you exhale, lead the Qi to the surface of the skin.

### 3.    Regulating the Mind:

In Qigong, the mind is considered the general who directs the battle against sickness. After all, it is your mind which manages all of your thinking and activity. Therefore, a clear, calm mind is very important so that you can judge clearly and accurately. In addition, your attention must also be concentrated. Your mind can generate an EMF (an electromagnetic force or "voltage") which causes your Qi to circulate. The more you concentrate, the more strongly you can lead the Qi.

When you have a calm and concentrated mind, you will be able to feel and sense the problem correctly. Therefore, when you practice Qigong for your arthritis you must learn how to bring your mind inward so that you can understand the situation, and you must know how to use your concentrated attention to lead the Qi.

### 4.    Regulating the Qi:

Once you have regulated your body, breathing, and mind, you will be in a good position to start regulating your Qi, and will be be able to lead your Qi anywhere in your body to make repairs.

### 5.    Regulating the Spirit:

The final key to Qigong is raising your spirit of vitality. Good morale or fighting spirit is necessary to win the war against illness. When your spirit is high, your willpower is strong, your mind is firm, and your patience can last a long time. In addition, when your spirit is high your emotions are under control and your wisdom mind can stimulate the Qi to circulate in the body more efficiently. This will significantly reduce the time of healing.

You should now have a clear idea of how to practice most efficiently. During the course of your practice you should frequently remind yourself of these key requirements. If you would like to learn more about the keys to Qigong practice, you may refer to the YMAA book: "The Root of Chinese Chi Kung." In the next section we will introduce several Qigong exercises which can be used to strengthen and maintain the health of the internal organs. The third section will discuss Qigong massage and cavity press for arthritis. Finally, the fourth section will introduce many Qigong exercises which can rebuild the strength of the joints.

### 4-2. Qigong for Strengthening the Internal Organs

Your internal organs are the foundation of your health. Most deaths are due to the malfunction or failure of the internal organs.

In order to be healthy and avoid degeneration, your organs need to have the correct amount of Qi circulating smoothly through them.

The internal organs manage the energy in our bodies, and carry out a variety of physical processes. When any organ starts to malfunction, the Qi circulation in the body will be disrupted, and the production of hormones will be affected. This state can result in a variety of disorders, including gouty arthritis.

In this section we would like to introduce two types of Qigong practices which are commonly used to improve Qi circulation, especially around the internal organs. The first exercise is massaging the internal organs by moving the muscles inside the torso. If you would like to have more information on the theory behind this subject, please refer to the YMAA book "The Eight Pieces of Brocade."

The second type of Qigong practice is improving the Qi circulation around the internal organs by massaging either directly over the organs or on acupuncture cavities which are connected to the organs. This subject will be discussed in more detail in the YMAA book "Qigong Massage."

## Massaging the Internal Organs with Movement

All of the internal organs are surrounded by muscles. Except for some of the trunk muscles which we use constantly throughout the day, most of these muscles are ignored. According to Qigong theory, if you can bring your Yi (mind) to a muscle, you can lead Qi to energize it and move it. For example, if you decide you want to be able to wiggle your ears and keep trying, you will eventually be able to. It's the same with the internal muscles. This means that, if you practice becoming very calm and bringing your attention deeper and deeper into the center of your body, you will soon be able to feel and sense the structure and condition of the insides of your body. Once this happens you can use your mind to move the internal muscles and massage the internal organs.

The way to reach this goal is to start by using your trunk muscles to make the muscles deeper inside your body move. After you have practiced for a while, your mind will be able to reach deeper and feel other muscles as well. Once you are able to feel these muscles, you will be able to move them. With a bit more practice you will be able to control them while keeping them relaxed, and the movements will become natural, easy, and comfortable. Remember that the muscles have to be relaxed before the organs can be relaxed and before the Qi can circulate smoothly.

In this sub-section we will introduce the beginning steps of internal organ massage through trunk movement. After you are able to do these exercises easily and smoothly, you should continue to lead your mind deeper and deeper into your body and sense your organs.

It is a good idea to loosen up your trunk before starting these massaging movements. This will let you move more naturally and comfortably.

Figure 4-1.                              Figure 4-2.

### Loosening the Torso Muscles

The torso is the center of the whole body, and it contains the muscles which control the torso and also surround the internal organs. When the torso muscles are tense, the whole body will be tense and the internal organs will be compressed. This causes stagnation of the Qi circulation in the body and especially in the organs. For this reason, the torso muscles should be stretched and loosened up before any moving Qigong practice.

First, interlock your fingers and lift your hands up over your head while imagining that you are pushing upward with your hands and pushing downward with your feet (Figure 4-1). Do not tense your muscles, because this will constrict your body and prevent you from stretching. If you do this stretch correctly, you will feel the muscles in your waist area tensing slightly because they are being pulled simultaneously from the top and the bottom. Next, use your mind to relax even more, and stretch out a little bit more. After you have stretched for about ten seconds, turn your upper body to one side to twist the trunk muscles (Figure 4-2). Stay to the side for three to five seconds, turn your body to face forward and then turn to the other side. Stay there for three to five seconds. Repeat the upper body twisting three times, then tilt your upper body to the side and stay there for about three seconds (Figure 4-3), then tilt to the other side. Next, bend forward and touch your hands to the floor (Figure 4-4) and stay there for three to five seconds. Finally, squat down with your feet flat on the floor to stretch your ankles (Figure 4-5), and then lift your heels up to stretch the toes (Figure 4-6).

Figure 4-3.

Figure 4-4.

Figure 4-5.

Figure 4-6.

Repeat the entire process ten times. After you finish, the inside of your body should feel very comfortable and warm.

The torso is supported by the spine and the trunk muscles. Once you have stretched your trunk muscles, you can loosen up the torso. This also moves the muscles inside your body around, which

Figure 4-7.

moves and relaxes your internal organs. This, in turn, makes it possible for the Qi to circulate smoothly inside your body.

**a.  Massaging the Large Intestine, Small Intestine, Urinary Bladder, and Kidneys**

This exercise helps you to regain conscious control of the muscles in your abdomen. There are four major benefits to this abdominal exercise. First, when your Lower Dan Tian area is loose, the Qi can flow in and out easily. The Lower Dan Tian is the main residence of your Original Qi. The Qi in your Dan Tian can be led easily only when your abdomen is loose and relaxed. Second, when the abdominal area is loose, the Qi circulation in the large and small intestines will be smooth, and they will be able to absorb nutrients and eliminate waste efficiently. If your body does not eliminate effectively, the absorption of nutrients will be hindered, and you may become sick. Third, when the abdominal area is loose, the Qi in the kidneys will circulate smoothly and the Original Essence stored there can be converted more efficiently into Qi. In addition, when the kidney area is loose, the kidney Qi can be led downward and upward to nourish the entire body. Fourth, these exercises eliminate Qi stagnation in the lower back, healing and preventing lower back pain.

To practice this exercise, stand with your feet a comfortable distance apart and your knees slightly bent. As you get more used to this exercise and your legs become stronger, bend your knees a little bit more. Without moving your thighs or upper body, use the waist muscles to move the abdomen around in a horizontal circle (Figure 4-7). Circle in one direction about ten times, and then in the other direction about ten times. If you hold one hand over your Lower Dan Tian and the other on your sacrum you may be able to focus your attention better on the area you want to control.

In the beginning you may have difficulty making your body move the way you want it to, but if you keep practicing you will quickly learn how to do it. Once you can do the movement comfortably, make the circles larger and larger. Naturally, this will cause the muscles to tense somewhat and inhibit the Qi flow, but the more you practice the sooner you will be able to relax again. After you have practiced for a while and can control your waist muscles easily, start making the circles smaller, and also start using your Yi to lead the Qi from the Dan Tian to move in these circles. The final goal is to have only a slight physical movement, but a strong movement of Qi.

When you practice, concentrate your mind on your abdomen and inhale and exhale deeply and smoothly. Remember that breathing deep does not mean breathing heavily. When you breathe deep, keep the diaphragm and the muscles surrounding the lungs relaxed. Inhale to lead the Qi into the center of the body and exhale to lead the Qi out through the skin.

**b.  Massaging the Stomach, Liver, Spleen, Gall Bladder, and Kidneys**

Beneath your diaphragm is your stomach, to the right are your liver and gall bladder, and to the left is your spleen, and in the back are your kidneys. Once you can comfortably do the circular movement in your lower abdomen, change the movement from horizontal to vertical, and extend it up to your diaphragm. The easiest way to loosen the area around the diaphragm is to use a wave-like motion between the perineum and the diaphragm (Figure 4-8). You may find it helpful when you practice this to place one hand on your Lower Dan Tian and your other hand above it with the thumb on the solar plexus. Use a forward and backward wave-like motion, flowing up to the diaphragm and down to the perineum and back. While you do this, inhale deeply when the motion is starting at the perineum and exhale as it reaches the diaphragm. Practice ten times.

Next, continue the movement while turning your body slowly to one side and then to the other (Figure 4-9). This will slightly tense the muscles on one side and loosen them on the other, which will massage the internal organs. Repeat ten times.

This exercise loosens the muscles around the stomach, liver, gall bladder, spleen, and kidneys, and therefore improves the Qi circulation there. It also trains you in using your mind to lead Qi from your Lower Dan Tian upward to the solar plexus area.

**c.  Massaging the Lungs and Heart**

This exercise loosens up the chest and helps to regulate and improve the Qi circulation in the lungs. According to the theory of the five phases in Chinese medicine, the lungs belong to the element Metal while the heart belongs to the element Fire. Metal is able to cool down Fire, and the lungs are able to regulate the Qi of the heart.

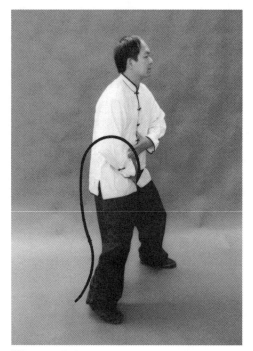

Figure 4-8.                         Figure 4-9.

The heart is the most vital organ, and its condition is closely related to our life and death. If there is too much Qi in the heart (when it is too Yang), you speed up its degeneration and become prone to heart attacks. For this reason, Qigong places great emphasis on using the lungs to regulate the Qi in the heart. If we know how to relax the lungs and keep the Qi circulating in them smoothly, they will be able to regulate the heart more efficiently.

After loosening up the center portion of your body, extend the movement up to your chest. The wave-like movement starts in the abdomen, moves through the stomach and up to the chest. You may find it easier to feel the movement if you hold one hand on your abdomen and the other lightly touching your chest (Figure 4-10). After you have done the movement ten times, extend the movement to your shoulders (Figure 4-11). Inhale when you move your shoulders backward and exhale when you move them forward. The inhalation and exhalation should be as deep as comfortably possible, and the entire chest should be very loose. Repeat the motion ten times.

## 2.  Massaging the Internal Organs with your Hands

Using the hands to massage the internal organs is a natural human instinct, and we do it whenever we feel pain or Qi stagnation in or near an organ. For example, if you have diarrhea and feel pain in your abdomen, you naturally massage yourself with your hand. Or if you overeat you automatically stroke or rub your stomach with your palms to ease the pain.

According to Chinese medicine, in the center of each palm is a cavity or gate called the "Laogong" (Figure 4-12) which is used to

Figure 4-10.

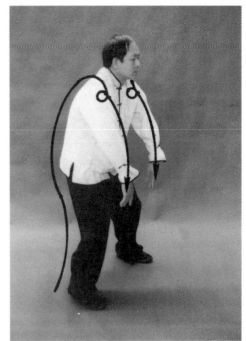

Figure 4-11.

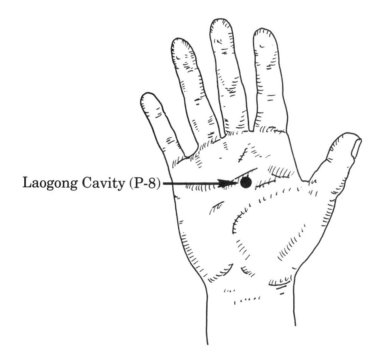

Figure 4-12. Laogong Cavity

regulate the Qi of the heart whenever the Qi flow is too strong. Unless you are sick, the Qi in the heart is normally more positive than is necessary, especially in the summertime. When you are excited or nervous, even more Qi accumulates around the heart.

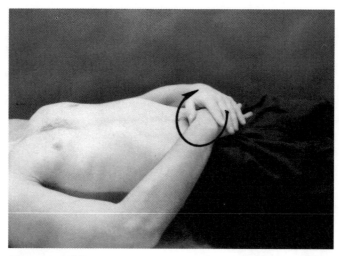

Figure 4-13.

When this happens, the centers of your palms will feel warm and will often sweat.

Since the Qi in the center of the palm is always strong, you can use this Qi to help the stagnant organ Qi to flow smoothly. Chinese physicians and Qigong practitioners have developed a number of ways of using the hands to improve the Qi circulation in the internal organs. In this section we will introduce a few common ones that can be practiced easily by anyone. It is not true that only an expert can heal people with his hands. Anyone can do it if they know how.

**a. Abdomen**

To massage your abdomen and regulate the Qi circulation in your large and small intestines, place one hand on top of the other on your lower abdomen (Figure 4-13). If you are right-handed, it is better if you place your right hand on the bottom and the left hand on the top. Naturally, if you are left-handed, place the left hand on the bottom. The reason for this is quite simple: the Qi is strongest in the hand you use most often, and it is easier for you to lead the Qi from it.

When you massage your abdomen, it is best if you lie down so that your lower body is relaxed and the Qi can circulate more easily and smoothly. Hold you hand lightly against the skin and gently circle your hands clockwise, which is the direction of movement within the large intestine (Figure 4-13). Circling in the other direction would hinder the natural movements of peristalsis. Massage until you feel warm and comfortable deep inside your body.

As you massage, your breathing should be relaxed, deep, and comfortable. Place your mind a few inches under your palms. The mind will then be able to lead the Qi inward to smooth out Qi and blood stagnation.

**b. Liver, Stomach, Spleen, and Gall Bladder**

In Qigong massage for the internal organs, the liver, stomach, spleen, and the gall bladder are usually included in the same tech-

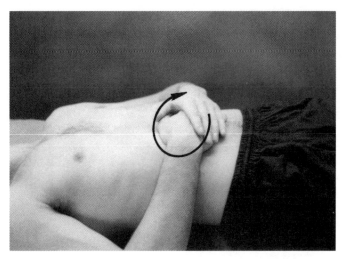

Figure 4-14.

niques because they are all located in the middle of the front of the body. Maintaining healthy Qi circulation in an organ requires not only that the circulation in the organ itself be smooth, but also that the circulation between the organs be smooth. Therefore, when you massage these four internal organs, you should treat them as one instead of four.

Hold your hands as you did when massaging the lower abdomen, only now place them above the navel. Experience has shown that clockwise is again more effective than counterclockwise (Figure 4-14). It is easiest to do this massage when you are lying down. It is also best if you have someone else to massage you, because it is then easiest for you to relax. Massage until you feel warm inside.

### c.  Kidneys

Chinese medicine considers the kidneys to be perhaps the most important internal organs. The kidneys affect how the other organs function, so almost all forms of Qigong place heavy emphasis on keeping them healthy.

To massage your own kidneys, close your hands into fists and place the thumb/index finger sides on your kidneys. Gently circle both fists until the kidneys are warm. In the summer, when your kidneys are normally too Yang, it is desirable to dissipate some of the Qi. This can be done by circling your right hand clockwise and your left hand counterclockwise (Figure 4-15). This leads the Qi to the sides of your body. However, when you massage your kidneys in the wintertime, when the kidney Qi is normally deficient (too Yin), then you should reverse the direction and lead the Qi to the center of your back to nourish the kidneys. As usual, the breathing and the mind are important keys to successful practice.

There are other methods of improving the Qi circulation in the kidneys. One of the most common ones is to massage the bottoms of

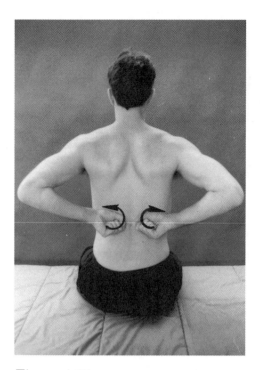

Figure 4-15.

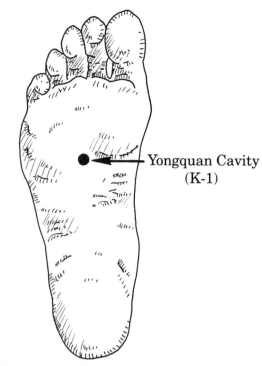

Figure 4-16. Yongquan Cavity

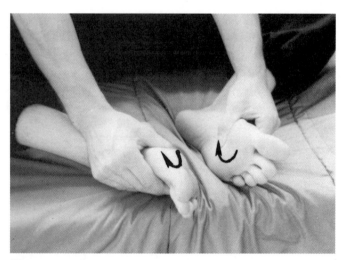

Figure 4-17.

your feet. There is a Qi gate in the front center of each sole which is called "Yongquan" (Bubbling Well)(Figure 4-16). Massaging these two cavities will stimulate the Qi circulation in the kidneys and help to regulate them (Figure 4-17).

**d.  Lungs**

As mentioned earlier, in the theory of the five elements the lungs belong to Metal while the heart belongs to Fire. According to this theory, the Metal lungs can be used to regulate the heart Fire just as metal can absorb heat. If you pay attention carefully you will

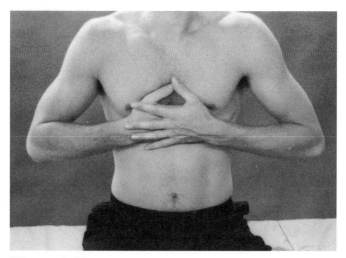

Figure 4-18.

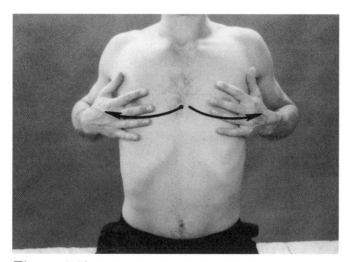

Figure 4-19.

notice that when you feel heat around your heart due to excitement or even depression, you will normally thrust out your chest and greatly expand your lungs while inhaling. Doing this a few times reduces the pressure and the feeling of heat in the heart.

To do Qigong massage for your lungs, place both hands on the center of your chest just above the solar plexus (Figure 4-18). Inhale deeply, and then exhale while lightly pushing both hands to the sides (Figure 4-19). Do this until your lungs feel relaxed and comfortable. This massage is also good for the heart.

### e. Heart

Qigong teachers do not normally encourage students to massage their own hearts unless they are fairly advanced in skill. The heart is the most vital organ, and if you mistreat it you are in big trouble.

When you massage your heart, unlike all the other internal organs, you cannot place your mind on it. If you do place your mind

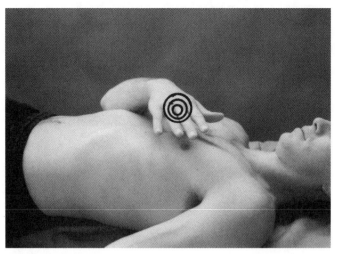

Figure 4-20.

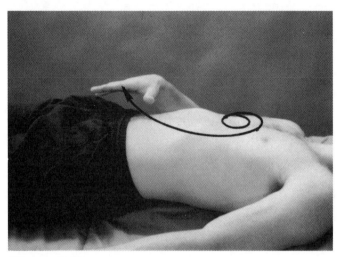

Figure 4-21.

on your heart you will lead more Qi to it and make it even more positive. You may have noticed that when your heart is beating fast after exercising, if you pay attention to your heartbeat it will start beating even faster. A person who is prone to heart attacks can possibly bring one on by paying too much attention to his heart. If your heart is beating too hard, the best thing is to pay attention to your lungs and breathe deeply and gently. After only a few breaths your heart will slow down and regain its regular pace.

Therefore, when you massage your heart, your mind should not be on your heart. Instead, keep your mind on the movement of your hands. To massage your heart, place your right hand over your heart at least three inches away from your chest (Figure 4-20). Move your hand in a small clockwise circle, and gradually increase the size of the circle. This takes the Qi in the heart and spreads it out around the chest. Finally, lead the Qi by the liver and down the right leg (Figure 4-21).

### f. Testicles

Massaging the testicles increases the production of hormones. According to Chinese Muscle/Tendon Changing and Marrow/Brain Washing Qigong (Yi Jin Jing and Xi Sui Jing), massaging the testicles correctly will increase hormone production and also increase the amount of Qi led upward to the brain. Other effects are increasing the amount of Qi stored in the body and strengthening the immune system. There are many ways to massage the testicles. For example, you may hold the testicles gently between your palms and circle your hands. You may also simply hold them in your hand and gently press and rub them. This subject is discussed in more detail in the YMAA book "Muscle/Tendon Changing and Marrow/Brain Washing Chi Kung."

### 4-3. Massage and Cavity Press (Acupressure)

Massage and cavity press are often used at the same time in treating arthritis. Massage is generally used first to loosen up the muscles and tendons around the joint and to increase the Qi circulation. Massage lets the power of the cavity press penetrate deeper into the joint.

In this section we will introduce some of the more common and easy-to-learn techniques. Many of them you can do to yourself, although the majority, such as those done on the neck and the spine, need to be done by someone else. Before we discuss how to massage the individual joints and the location of the cavities, we would first like to mention one important point: when you are giving massage or cavity press treatments, you should not over-stimulate the area or cavity (pressure point). Over-stimulation can only cause pain and generate further stagnation of the Qi and blood. In addition, too much pressure can further injure a joint which may be starting to heal. The purpose of massage and cavity press is to increase the Qi and blood circulation, and anything which causes pain is incorrect. Next, we will introduce some of the basic massage and cavity press techniques.

### Basic Massage and Cavity Press Techniques:

The first basic technique for massaging joints is to place a hand on the joint and rub gently back and forth or in circles until the area is warm (Figure 4-22). As the joint gets looser, you may increase the pressure as you rub so that the power penetrates deeper into the joint.

The second technique uses the middle joints of the fingers to massage. Hold the area you are massaging with the middle knuckles of your fingers, and be sure not to press the thumbs in and cause bruises (Figure 4-23). You want to feel the muscles and tendons, so apply gentle pressure and penetrate in with your mind. Do not rub the skin. Instead, move your fingers back and forth and in circles to massage the muscles and tendons beneath the skin.

The third technique uses the thumb to rub or press and circle along the muscles and tendons of the joints (Figure 4-24). The other four

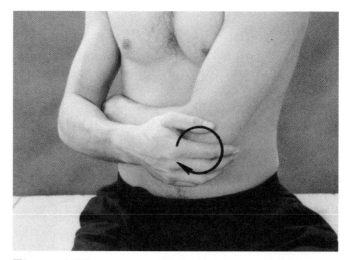

Figure 4-22.

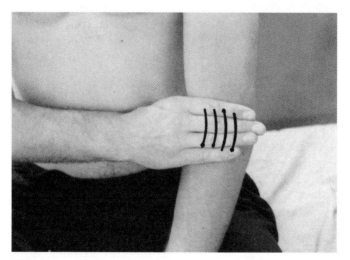

Figure 4-23.

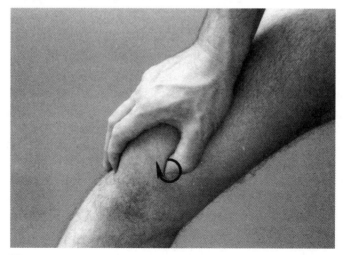

Figure 4-24.

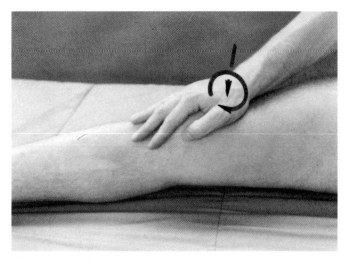

Figure 4-25.

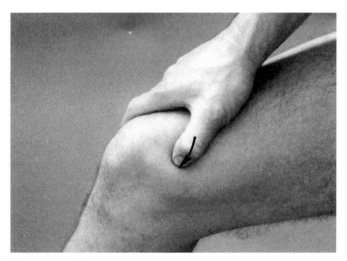

Figure 4-26.

fingers are usually used to stabilize the thumb. This technique is used to increase the Qi circulation and to lead the Qi away from the joints.

The last basic technique uses the base of the palm (Figure 4-25). Press your palm lightly inward to contact the muscles and tendons that you want to massage, and then move your palm in circles. Do not rub the skin. After you have loosened one area, follow the muscle and tendon away from the joint and repeat the procedure. Adjust the pressure to control the depth of the massage and stimulate the various levels of muscle and tendon.

In cavity press you use a fingertip to press directly on the cavity with deep concentration. The thumb press (Figure 4-26) is usually used most, however the index finger (Figure 4-27) and middle finger (Figure 4-28) are also used. Occasionally, when greater pressure is desired, the index and middle fingers are used together (Figure 4-29). Frequently, pressure is applied with a circular motion. If you are using your right hand, a clockwise motion usually nourishes the

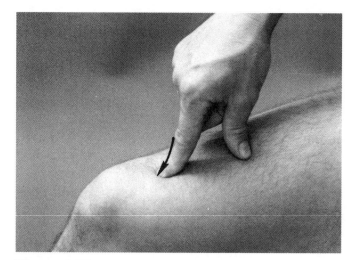

Figure 4-27.

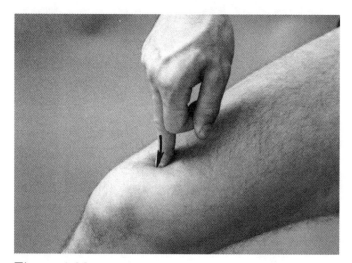

Figure 4-28.

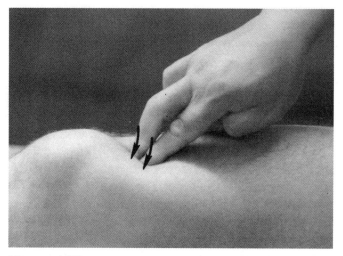

Figure 4-29.

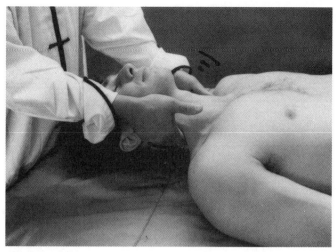

Figure 4-30.

cavity while a counterclockwise one lowers the Qi level. This is because a clockwise motion leads your Yi (mind) forward and a counterclockwise one leads your Yi back. Naturally, if you are using your left hand, you circle counterclockwise to lead the Qi forward and clockwise to lead it backward. Remember, your Yi is the key to leading the Qi forward and backward through your fingers.

## A. The Neck and Spine
### a. Neck
#### Massage:

The main purpose of massaging the neck is to loosen up the two main muscles in the back of the neck and to increase the Qi circulation. The best posture for a neck massage is lying on your back with the massager above your head (Figure 4-30). An alternate way is sitting with the head pushed slightly back to relax the muscles. Starting at the top of the neck, rub downward with your thumbs. You may do this yourself (Figure 4-31) or have a partner do it for you (Figure 4-32). Next, use the middle joints of your fingers to gently squeeze the muscles and move them around. Again, it is easier and more comfortable if someone else can do it for you (Figure 4-33).

#### Cavity Press:

There are six cavities which can be used to stimulate the Qi circulation deep in the neck: Fengfu (Gv-16), Yamen (Gv-15), the two Fengchi (GB-20) cavities, and the two Tianzhu (B-10) cavities (Figure 4-34). The thumb or index finger are most commonly used. When doing this on yourself, first concentrate your mind, and then gently press with a finger while keeping your neck relaxed. Press for three to five seconds and then let up. Five to ten presses are usually needed for proper stimulation. After the cavity press, place your attention deep inside the vertebrae and move your head around a few times.

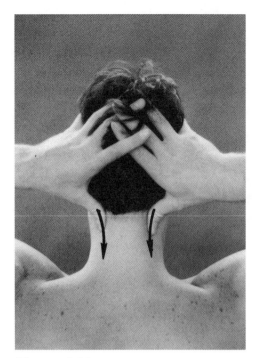

Figure 4-31.

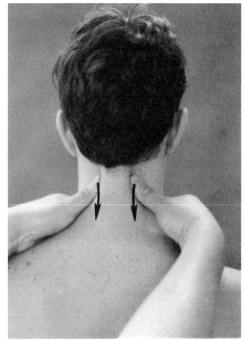

Figure 4-32.

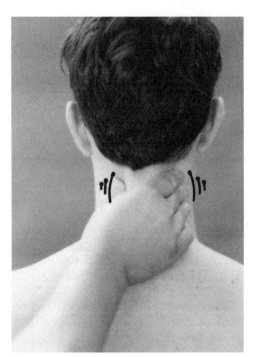

Figure 4-33.

**b.  Spine**
**Massage:**
Obviously, you need to have someone else massage your back.
Before you can loosen up the spine, you must first loosen up the

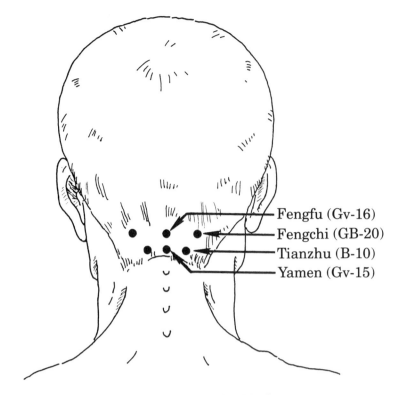

Figure 4-34. Cavities on the Neck

Fengfu (Gv-16)
Fengchi (GB-20)
Tianzhu (B-10)
Yamen (Gv-15)

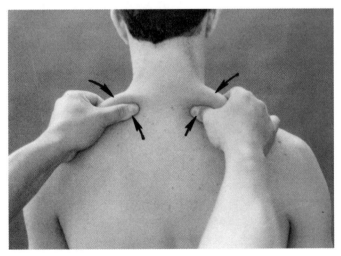

Figure 4-35.

trunk muscles. Therefore, start at the neck and gradually work downward. Loosen the neck muscles as explained above, then grab and gently squeeze the muscles between the neck and the shoulders (Figure 4-35). This will help lead the Qi from the neck downward and spread it out across your back. Next, use the base of your palm (Figure 4-36) or the edge of your palm (Figure 4-37) to press the trunk muscles, moving down with a circular massaging motion. Massage from the neck down to the waist five to ten times. Do not

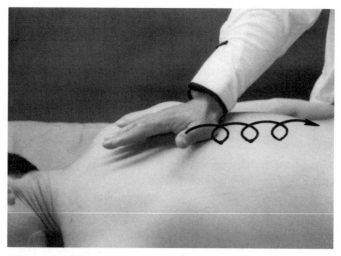

Figure 4-36.

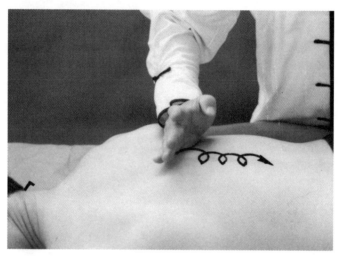

Figure 4-37.

massage upward, because it will lead the Qi in the wrong direction and cause stagnation.

Once you have finished the circular pressing massage, place one hand on top of the other and press down on each joint in the spine. Do not press on the neck. Be sure that you press on the joints, and not on the vertebrae. The purpose is to bend and loosen the joints a little (Figure 4-38). Press in coordination with the patient's breathing. Place your hands in position and ask your patient to inhale deeply and then exhale. When your patient is exhaling, press down. How hard you press depends on the patient. Start with light power and observe the patient's reaction. If he or she holds their breath and tenses their muscles, then you are pressing too hard.

**Cavity Press:**
Starting on the neck, press your thumbs into the gaps between the joints (Figure 4-39). When you have reached the tailbone, press

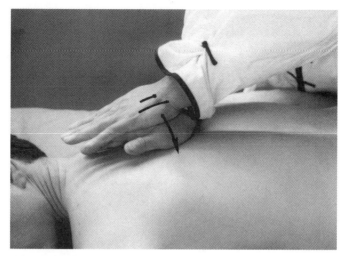

Figure 4-38.

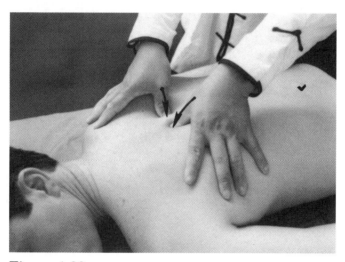

Figure 4-39.

the Shangliao (B-31), Baihuanshu (B-30), Zhibian (B-49), and Huantiao (GB-30) cavities to lead the Qi to the hips (Figures 4-40 and 4-41). Finally, use the base of the palm to gently massage the sacrum for three minutes (Figure 4-42).

After you have finished pressing on the sides of the spine, repeat the procedure, only now press about two inches away from the spine. Figure 4-40 shows the cavities which should be pressed. After pressing, again use the palm to rub the trunk muscles, pushing to the sides and also downward (Figure 4-43). This procedure leads stagnant Qi sideways and downward away from the spine.

**c. Waist**
   **Massage:**
   After you have massaged and loosened up the back, then start on the kidneys. Good Qi circulation in the kidneys is very important. When it is abnormal, the surrounding area will also be affected.

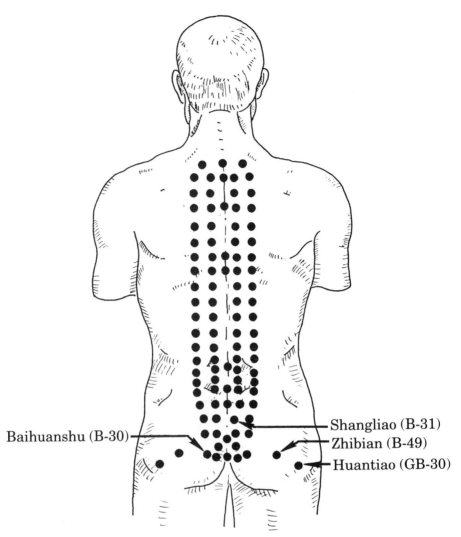

Figure 4-40. Cavities on the Spine

Baihuanshu (B-30)

Shangliao (B-31)

Zhibian (B-49)

Huantiao (GB-30)

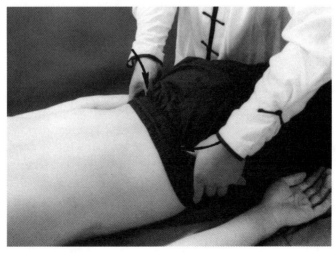

Figure 4-41.

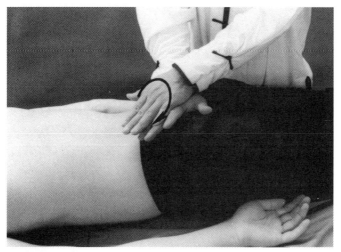

Figure 4-42.

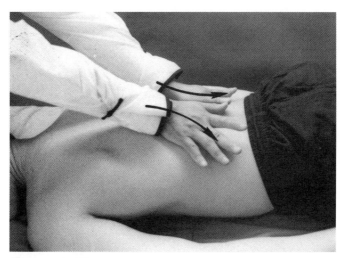

Figure 4-43.

To massage the kidneys, use the same circular motion discussed earlier. It is best to have someone else massage your kidneys. If you are massaging someone, you may also press gently down on the kidneys with your palms, and then release the pressure (Figure 4-44). Do this about ten times and you will feel the tension in the kidneys release and the Qi circulation improve. Finally, use both palms to push from the kidneys to the sides of the body and also downward to the hips.

Next, press and release with your palms on the joint between the sacrum and the first vertebra about ten times (Figure 4-45), and then push to the sides and to the hips to lead the Qi there (Figure 4-46). An alternative way is to place your hands on the kidneys or waist and move your hands in circles. Keep your hands in contact with the skin so that they lightly brush it, but don't let them rub the skin (Figure 4-47). Use very little pressure, so that the patient is comfortable and doesn't feel any pain.

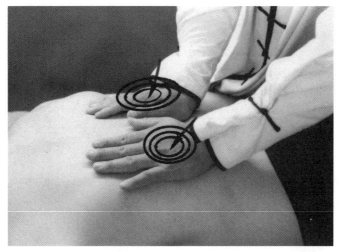

Figure 4-44.

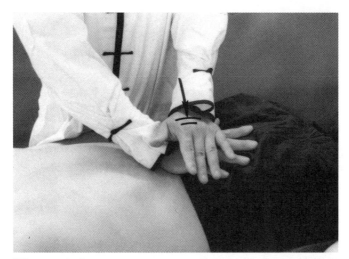

Figure 4-45.

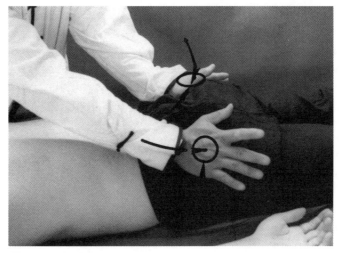

Figure 4-46.

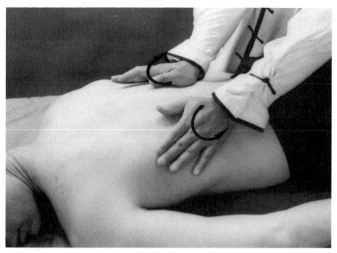

Figure 4-47.

**Cavity Press:**

After you finished the massage, you can then use your thumbs to press the cavities shown in Figure 4-48. Start with Mingmen (Gv-4), and move down to Yaoyangquan (Gv-3), Shiqizhuixia (M-BW-25), Yaoqi (M-BW-29), and finally Yaoshu (Gv-2). Press each cavity three to five times, about three seconds each time. Next, press Sanjiaoshu (B-22), Shenshu (B-23), Qihaishu (B-24), Shangliao (B-31), Baihuanshu (B-30), Zhibian (B-49), and Huantiao (GB-30) cavities the same way to lead the Qi to the hips. Experience will teach you the appropriate pressing techniques and how to apply power. The more you practice, the more easily you will be able to penetrate with your power, and the more effective your cavity press will be.

## B.   Joints in the Limbs

In this section we will discuss a few of the techniques used for massaging the joints in the limbs. Once you are familiar with them, you may use the same theory to come up with others. Remember that the goal of massage is to loosen up the muscles and tendons and to increase the Qi circulation.

**Massage:**

Small joints such as in the fingers and toes can be held between the thumb and index finger while you apply circular pressure with the thumb (Figure 4-49). Move from one point to another until you have massaged the entire joint.

With the bigger joints - wrists, knees, elbows, and shoulders - place your palm over the joint and massage in a circular motion until the joint is warm (Figure 4-50). You can then press and circle in particular areas with a finger or thumb to stimulate the Qi circulation (Figure 4-51).

It is usually easier to have someone else massage your shoulder or hip. If you are the person massaging, use your palm (Figure 4-52), the edge of the palm (Figure 4-53), or the knuckles (Figure 4-54)

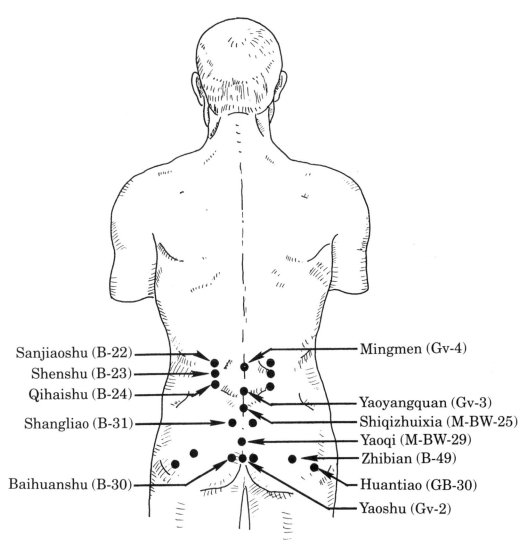

Sanjiaoshu (B-22)
Shenshu (B-23)
Qihaishu (B-24)
Shangliao (B-31)

Baihuanshu (B-30)

Mingmen (Gv-4)

Yaoyangquan (Gv-3)
Shiqizhuixia (M-BW-25)
Yaoqi (M-BW-29)
Zhibian (B-49)
Huantiao (GB-30)
Yaoshu (Gv-2)

Figure 4-48. Cavities on the Waist

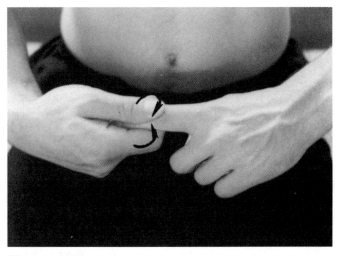

Figure 4-49.

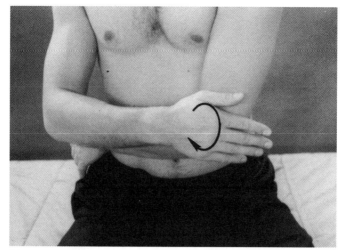

Figure 4-50.

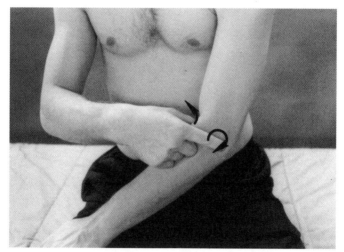

Figure 4-51.

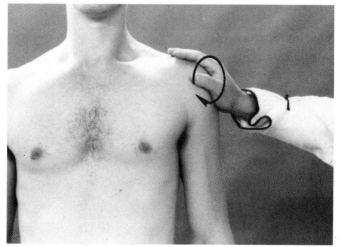

Figure 4-52.

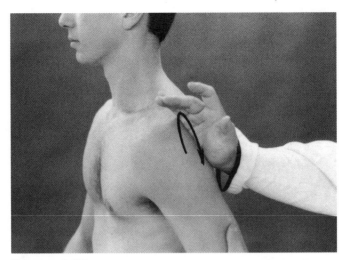

Figure 4-53.

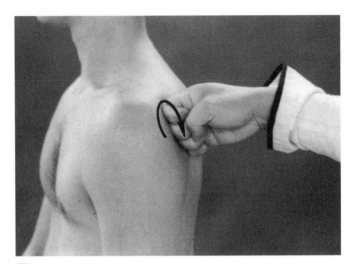

Figure 4-54.

to press in and rub. These are only a few of the many techniques which can be used to massage the joints and increase the Qi circulation. As you practice you may discover many other ways to let your power penetrate deep into the joints.

Next we will discuss the cavities or pressure points which are commonly used for cavity press. Some of them are not actually acupuncture cavities, but rather places where finger pressure can easily penetrate deep into the joints.

**Cavity Press:**
**Arms:**
a. Hands (Fingers and Palms)(Figure 4-55)
Hegu (LI-4), Sanjian (LI-3), Baxie (M-UE-22), Sifeng (M-UE-9), Shangbaxie (M-UW-50), Shaoshang (L-11), Shaoze (SI-1), Laogong (P-8), and Zhongzhu (TB-3).
b. Wrists (Figure 4-56)

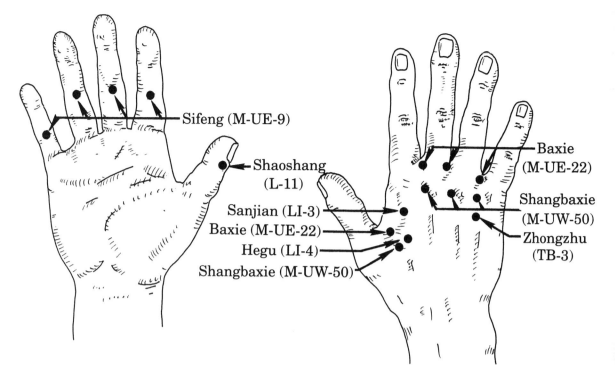

Figure 4-55. Cavities on the Hand

Yangchi (TB-4), Yanglao (SI-6), Yangxi (LI-5), Taiyuan (L-9), Daling (P-7), Shenmen (H-7), and Tongli (H-5).

**c.** Elbows (Figure 4-57)

Quchi (LI-11), Shousanli (LI-10), Chize (L-5), Quze (P-3), Shaohai (H-3), and Xiaohai (SI-8).

**d.** Shoulders (Figure 4-58)

Jianqian (M-UE-48), Jugu (LI-16), Jianliao (TB-14), Jubi (N-UE-10), Taijian (N-UE-11), Biano (LI-14), and Jianjing (GB-21).

**Legs:**

**a.** Toes and Feet (Figure 4-59)

Chongyang (S-42), Foot-Linqi (GB-41), Taichong (Li-3), Xiangu (S-43), Zhiyin (B-67), Bafeng (M-LE-8), Dadun (Li-1), Yinbai (Sp-1), and Yongchuan (K-1).

**b.** Ankles (Figure 4-60)

Jiexi (S-41), Zhaohai (K-6), Taixi (K-3), Kunlun (B-60), and Shenmai (B-62).

**c.** Knees (Figure 4-61)

Dubi (S-35 or M-LE-16), Heding (M-LE-27), Xiyangquan (GB-33), Weizhong (B-54), Weiyang (B-53), and Weishang (N-LE-25).

**d.** Hips (Figure 4-62)

Femur-Juliao (GB-29) and Huantiao (GB-30).

## 4-4. Qigong Exercises for Arthritis

Before introducing the Qigong exercises, we would first like to discuss the best time to practice Qigong. Experience indicates that the

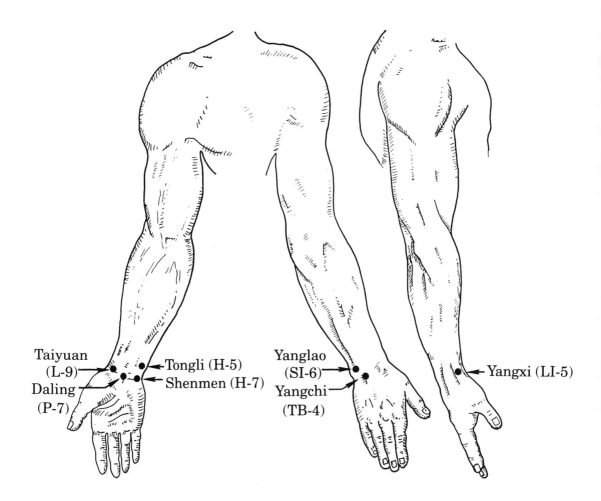

Figure 4-56. Cavities on the Wrist

best time is in the early morning. The pain and stiffness of arthritis are most severe in the early morning because the Qi is most stagnant. If you can do some massage and some Qigong, you should be able to remove the stagnation and lessen the discomfort for the rest of the day. Therefore, in the early morning you should gently and lightly massage the joints until they are warm and the Qi circulation has increased, and then gradually and gently start the Qigong exercises.

You should also do the exercises right before you go to bed to smooth out any Qi stagnation. This will speed up the repair and healing of the joints while you sleep, and also lessen pain and stiffness the next morning. If you are able, you may add another practice session in the afternoon. Normally, your Qi is the strongest in the afternoon. You may take advantage of this to do Qigong exercises and lead Qi to the joints. Naturally, if you have the time, you may do the Qigong exercises whenever you can.

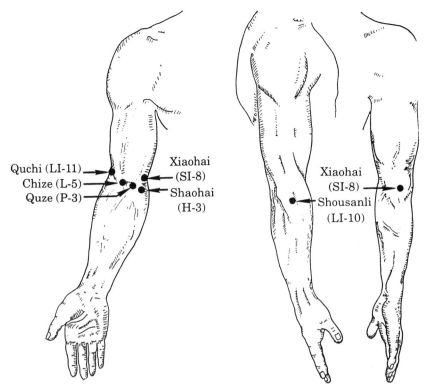

Figure 4-57. Cavities on the Elbow

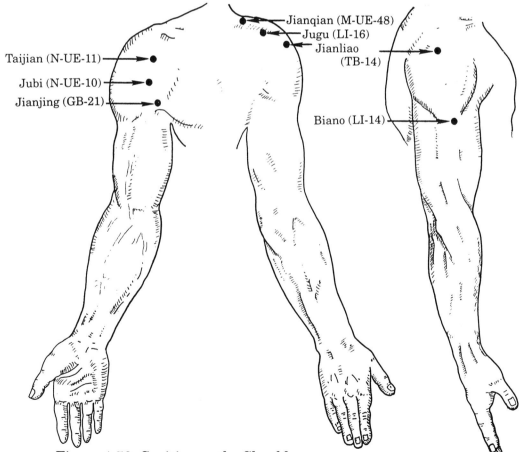

Figure 4-58. Cavities on the Shoulder

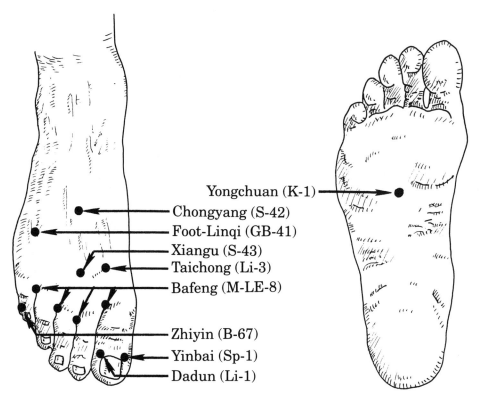

Yongchuan (K-1)

Chongyang (S-42)
Foot-Linqi (GB-41)
Xiangu (S-43)
Taichong (Li-3)
Bafeng (M-LE-8)

Zhiyin (B-67)
Yinbai (Sp-1)
Dadun (Li-1)

Figure 4-59. Cavities on the Foot

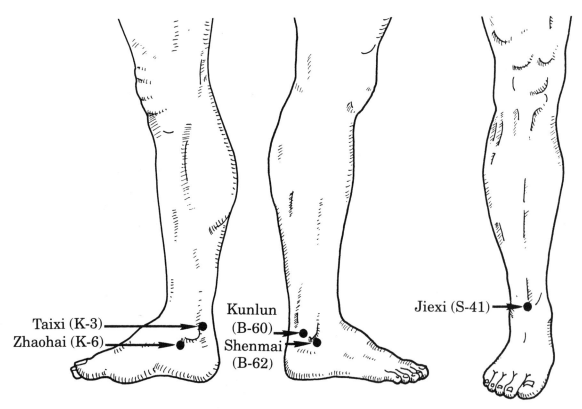

Taixi (K-3)
Zhaohai (K-6)

Kunlun (B-60)
Shenmai (B-62)

Jiexi (S-41)

Figure 4-60. Cavities on the Ankle

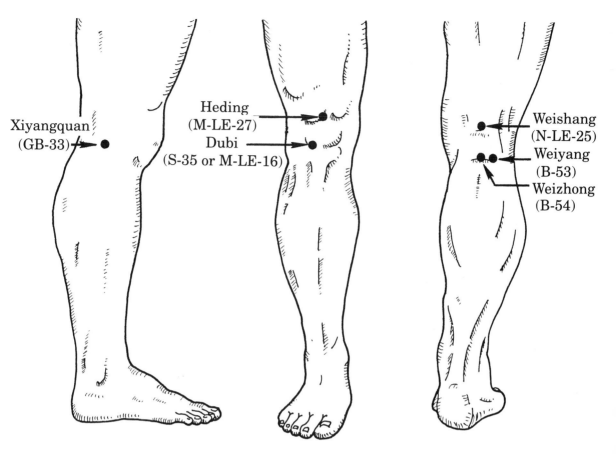

Figure 4-61. Cavities on the Knee

There are a few things that you should be aware of. First, when the joint is inflamed you should not get involved in heavy Qigong exercise. Gently massage the joint to increase the Qi circulation and then do some light and easy exercises. Second, when you have the least pain and stiffness, take advantage of the opportunity and practice a little more than usual. Third, do not overdo it. The way to judge this is that if about two hours after practice you still feel significant pain, then it was probably too much. The next time you should reduce the number of repetitions. With a little experience you will soon be able to judge what is right for you. Practice a comfortable length of time, and gradually increase the number of repetitions. Fourth, you should minimize the stress directly on the affected joints. As mentioned earlier, the best and most effective way is to bring the practice into your daily life and let it become a habit.

In this section we will introduce a number of Qigong exercises which can be used to heal arthritis and rebuild the joints. Remember that the key to healing and regrowth is leading Qi to the joints and helping it to circulate smoothly there. The main way to do this is to really concentrate your attention on the area you are exer-

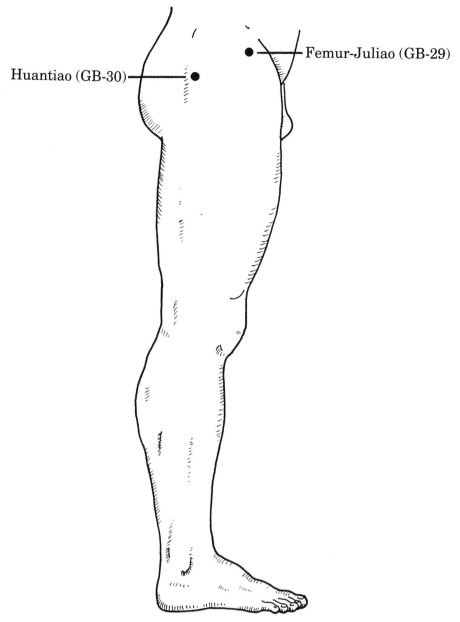

Huantiao (GB-30)

Femur-Juliao (GB-29)

Figure 4-62. Cavities on the Hip

cising. When you concentrate, your Yi (mind) leads Qi to the joint. Breathing calmly and deeply also helps you to lead the Qi inward into the organs, joints, and bone marrow. Once you have grasped these tricks, you will be able to use the Qigong movements to circulate Qi in the joint smoothly and strongly.

When you practice, you should wear warm clothing and avoid exposing your joints to cold air or wind. After you practice, you should cover the joints and keep them warm. Remember that everyone is different, and you have to use your common sense to judge what is best for you.

When you are just starting these Qigong exercises, remember that you should not focus on building up the muscles and tendons. If you do this, your concentration will cause them to tense. This will increase the pressure in the joint and may cause the bones to grind against each other, which will hinder the healing process. Furthermore, although exercising the muscles and tendons may lead Qi to the joints, if you exercise too strenuously you will cause tension, which will stagnate the Qi circulation. You should always remember that **THE KEY TO GOOD QIGONG IS USING THE MIND AND GENTLE MOVEMENTS TO LEAD QI TO THE JOINTS AND INCREASE SMOOTH QI CIRCULATION**.

Once you have repaired some of the joint damage, you can then gradually start to emphasize strengthening the muscles and tendons. When the joints, muscles, and tendons are healthy, you have cured the arthritis. Remember that the strength of the joints must be built slowly and gradually. Do not expect to rebuild them in one night, one week, or even a month. However, after three months of consistent practice you should start to see improvement.

**Qigong Exercises**
**A.  The Trunk:**
**Neck**
The neck is the passageway to the brain for the Qi and blood. The brain is the center of your whole being, so if the circulation of the Qi and blood is stagnant or blocked, your brain will not receive the proper nourishment. This causes dizziness, headache, and in the long term, memory loss and accelerated aging. Blockages of the circulation to the head are often caused by neck injuries or arthritis in the neck joints. You can see that, in order to keep your brain functioning healthily, the first step is to remove any blockages of the circulation in the neck. The next two exercises are commonly used in China for this purpose.

**i.   Look Left and Right (Zuo Gu You Pan)  左顧右盼**

This exercise can be done with the eyes open or closed, as long as you are able to concentrate your mind on your neck. Keep your mind calm, concentrate on what you are doing, and feel the movement of the joints. The more you concentrate, the deeper you will lead the Qi.

The exercise is very simple. Simply turn your head slowly from one side to the other (Figure 4-63). You may sit or stand. As you turn your head to the side, exhale, and as you turn your head back to the front, inhale. Keep your neck as relaxed as possible. Keep turning your head until your neck starts getting warm, which may take twenty to fifty turns.

**ii.  The Heaven Spins and the Earth Turns (Tian Xuan Di Zhuan)  天旋地轉**

After you have finished the head turning exercise, continue by rotating your head. Stay relaxed and concentrated. Simply rotate

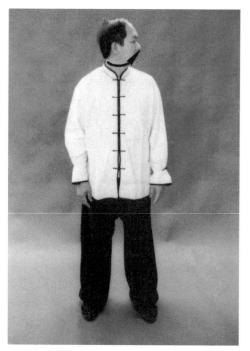

Figure 4-63.                    Figure 4-64.

your head clockwise about twenty to fifty times and then counter-clockwise another twenty to fifty times (Figure 4-64). Rotate your head the same number of times in both directions. When you have finished, close your eyes, keep your mind calm, and feel the Qi flowing in your neck area for a few minutes.

**Spine**

According to Chinese medicine there is a Qi vessel called the Governing Vessel (Du Mai) which follows the spine upward to the back of your head. Any problem with the spine can cause muscle tension, which, in turn, can cause stagnation of the Qi flow in the Governing Vessel. The Governing Vessel controls the six Yang primary Qi channels in the body (Large Intestine, Small Intestine, Triple Burner, Urinary Bladder, Gall Bladder, and Stomach channels). When there is any problem with the Qi circulation in the Governing Vessel, the six Yang primary channels and their related organs will also be affected.

Since any problem with your spine directly affects your health, Chinese Qigong pays a lot of attention to strengthening the spine and maintaining the Qi circulation in the back. The following movements are only some of the exercises which can be used to strengthen and maintain Qi circulation in the spine and back.

**i.    Large Dragon Moves Its Body (Da Long Ruan Shen)  大龍軟身**

This exercise is a wave-like movement which starts at the legs and flows upward to the sacrum and finishes at the neck (Figure 4-65). The movement can be from side to side and/or forward and

Figure 4-65.                    Figure 4-66.

backward. You may interlock your hands and move them along with your body. Keep your attention on your spine, where the movement is. You may also do this exercise sitting down, in which case you generate the movement in your abdomen and let it flow upward. The body remains as relaxed as possible. Practice from twenty to fifty times until the spine feels warm.

**ii.   Large Dragon Turns Its Body (Da Long Zhuan Shen)**　大龍轉身
Continue the wave movement described above, only now also start turning from side to side (Figure 4-66). The turning uses the trunk muscles to rotate the vertebrae, which increases the mobility of the spine.

**Waist**
Be very careful when you exercise your waist. Moving too vigorously can injure the lower back and spine, so proceed slowly and carefully. The following three Qigong exercises can improve Qi circulation around the waist.

**i.   Rotating the Waist (Niu Yao Xian Huo)**　扭腰現活
This is a very simple exercise. Keep your head and feet in place as you gently and smoothly move your waist in a circle (Figure 4-67). Circle ten to twenty times in one direction, and then do the same in the other direction. As you practice, pay attention to the waist area and try to feel the movement inside your body. When you can feel the movement of your spine it means that you are leading Qi to it and at the same time using the motion to circulate it.

Figure 4-67.                    Figure 4-68.

### ii.   Lion Rotates its Head (Shi Zi Yao Tou)  獅子搖頭

In this exercise, keep your legs and waist in place and swing your upper body in a circle (Figure 4-68). You may also do this exercise while sitting on a chair. Move in one direction ten to twenty times, and then move in the reverse direction the same number of times. Remember to move gently. Your mind is always the key to success.

### iii.   Bend and Straighten the Waist (Qian Gong Hou Ju) 前躬後鞠

This is one of the easiest Qigong exercises. In Chinese Wai Dan Qigong it is commonly used to massage the kidneys by tensing and relaxing the back muscles. It is also used to clear up waist problems and back pain. To do this exercise, simply relax your body as much as possible and bend forward. Stay bent over for about five seconds and then gently straighten up (Figure 4-69). Repeat ten to twenty times. Once your waist has regained its strength, you may increase the number of repetitions. As always, keep your mind on the area being exercised.

### B.   Limbs
### Arms:
### a.   Hands (Fingers and Palms)

Usually when you exercise your fingers, your palms are also involved. In addition, since they are all connected, whenever you exercise your hands you are also to some degree exercising your wrists.

Chinese physicians have found that people who use their hands and fingers a lot are sick less often than people who don't. The reason for this is very simple. There are six primary Qi channels which connect the fingers to six of your internal organs. Whenever

Figure 4-69.

Figure 4-70.

you work with your hands you build up Qi in those channels, and this Qi then flows into and nourishes the internal organs. There are many Qigong exercises for the hands. We will present four of them.

### i. Swimming Octopus (Zhang Yu You Shui) 章魚游水

This exercise also includes the wrists. Stretch your hands forward while spreading out the fingers (Figure 4-70), and then draw your wrists back while closing the fingers (Figure 4-71). Move your hands in and out, opening and closing the hands so that they look like a swimming octopus. If you wish, you may practice this one hand at a time. After doing this movement thirty to fifty times, your

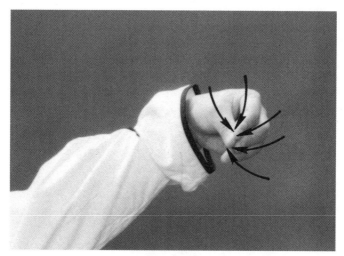

Figure 4-71.

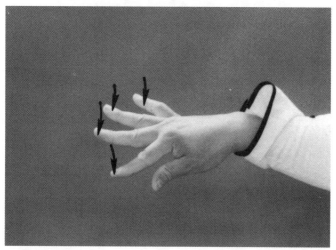

Figure 4-72.

fingers, palms, and wrists will usually feel very warm. Remember, when you practice your hands should remain as relaxed as possible, and your mind should be concentrated on them.

## ii. Flying Finger Waves Gong (Zhi Bo Xiang Gong)  指波翔功

This exercise is used by the crane style of Gongfu to strengthen the palms and the base of the fingers. Simply bend your thumbs and fingers one after the other and then straighten them one at a time, repeating the motion in a sort of wave (Figure 4-72). Only bend the knuckles closest to the hands. If you bend the other knuckles you will fail to develop the base of the fingers. After you have done twenty to fifty repetitions, your palms and the base of your fingers should feel very warm and perhaps a little sore. After practicing, relax your arms as much as possible to allow the Qi which has accumulated in your hands to circulate to your arms and body.

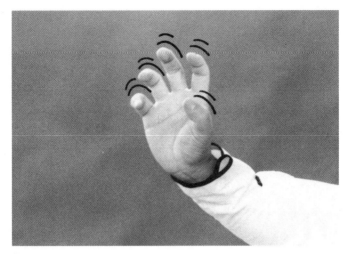

Figure 4-73.

Figure 4-74.

### iii. Tiger Claw Training (Hu Zhua Xing Gong) 虎爪行功

This exercise originated with the tiger claw style of Gongfu, and is more strenuous than the previous ones. This means that you should be more careful about how much tension you generate during practice. If your arthritis is very serious, you should probably not tense your muscles until your condition has improved, and then you should increase the tension very gradually.

To do this exercise, hold your hands like a tiger's paws (Figure 4-73) and gradually pull all of your fingers in to the center of the palms (Figure 4-74), and then open your hands again to the tiger's paw shape. After twenty to fifty repetitions, your fingers and palms should be very warm. When finished, relax your arms and allow the Qi to flow freely upward into your body.

### iv. Rolling the Taiji Ball (Zhuan Taiji Qiu) 轉太极球

In China, Taiji balls are well-known for their ability to cure many illnesses, such as irregular Qi circulation in the six primary

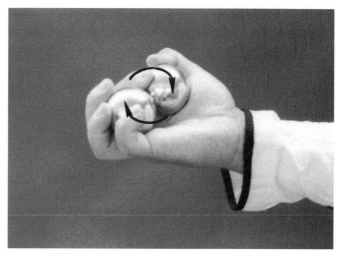

Figure 4-75.

channels, and also local problems such as arthritis. Many arthritis patients have used Taiji balls to cure arthritis in the fingers and palms and to strengthen their joints.

Martial Taiji practitioners do a variety of exercises with various sizes of balls. However, the balls used for treating arthritis in the hands and wrists usually have a diameter of about one and one-half inches. In ancient times the balls were made of wood. Nowadays, however, they are made of metal, which is stronger and lasts longer. Metal Taiji balls can be purchased in most Chinese department stores or martial art supplies stores.

Taiji ball training for arthritis in the hands is very simple. Hold two of the balls in one hand and move them in a circle with your fingers to rotate them (Figure 4-75). Your hands should feel warm after only five to ten minutes. If you are patient and practice three or four times a day, you should see improvement in your arthritic condition in only a few months.

Once your arthritis has improved, you may start rebuilding the strength of your muscles by increasing the tension in your hands as you do the following exercises.

**b. Wrists**
**i. Rotating the Wrists (Zhuan Wan) 轉腕**
Rotating your wrists is very simple - you just relax your wrists and move your hands in circles (Figure 4-76). Keep your attention on your wrists to feel the rotation and make it as smooth as possible. Keep rotating until your wrists are warm, and then reverse the rotation and do the same number of repetitions. It usually takes 300 or more rotations before your wrists start to feel warm, especially in the wintertime.

**ii. Rotating the Wrists with Interlocked Fingers (Jiao Zhi Zhuan Wan) 交指轉腕**
This exercise is similar to the previous one, only now the hands are interlocked and help each other. Lace your fingers together and

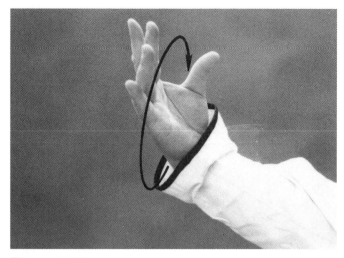

Figure 4-76.

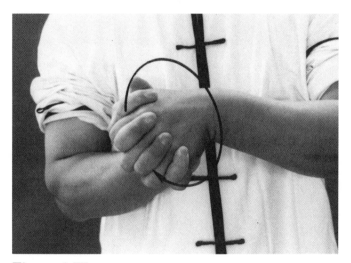

Figure 4-77.

move both hands in circles (Figure 4-77). Keep your attention on your wrists, and practice the same number of times in either direction. Once you have rebuilt your joints, this exercise can also be very helpful in rebuilding the tendons and muscles in your wrists. To do this, simply increase the tension on the wrists.

### iii. Rotating the Wrists while Holding Hands (Jiao Shou Zhuan Wan) 交手轉腕

This exercise is very similar to the previous one, only now, instead of interlocking your fingers, your hands are grasping each other (Figure 4-78). Again, keep your mind on your wrists and feel what is going on there. Once you have rebuilt the joints, you can increase the pressure to strengthen the tendons and muscles.

As you can see, the exercises are quite simple. You can easily discover other movements or exercises which lead Qi to the joints and

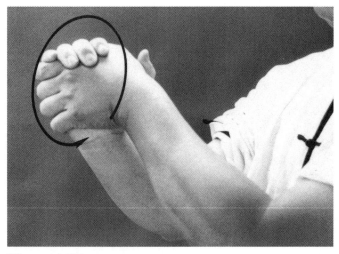

Figure 4-78.

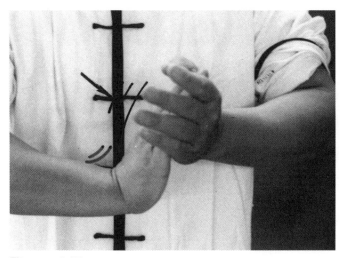

Figure 4-79.

increase their strength. For example, you can simply hold one hand steady and push it with the other one, and then relax. Push and relax until the wrist of the pushing hand starts to get warm (Figure 4-79).

**c. Elbows**
**i. Lifting Movement (Shang Ti Wan Zhou) 上提彎肘**
Extend your arms out in front of you with the palms up as if you were holding something (Figure 4-80). Raise your hands up to your face (Figure 4-81), and then lower them. Keep your mind on your elbows, and practice until they are warm. Then practice the same movement with the palms facing down. Once you are comfortable with this exercise, you can do it holding books or other light objects in your hands.

**ii. Sideward Movement (Nei Wai Wan Zhou) 内外彎肘**
Extend your arms to the sides with the palms facing upward (Figure 4-82). Keeping your elbows in place, move your hands in to

Figure 4-80.

Figure 4-81.

Figure 4-82.

Figure 4-83.

touch your chest (Figure 4-83) and then out again to the starting position. Keep your mind on your elbows and continue to practice until they are warm. Then turn your palms down and repeat the same movement. Once you are comfortable with the exercise you can hold light objects in your hands as you practice.

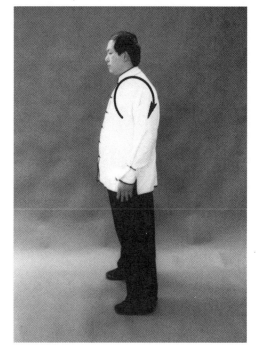

Figure 4-84.                    Figure 4-85.

### iii.  Rotating the Elbows (Zhuan Zhou)  轉肘

Hold your arms in front of you as if you were driving a car. Keeping your elbows in place, move your hands in circles (Figure 4-84). Start with 50 repetitions of an inward motion, and then 50 times in the other direction. Don't make the circles too big, as this will put too much tension on the tendons in the elbows.

### d.  Shoulders
### i.  Rotating the Shoulders (Song Jian)  聳肩

Use your shoulder muscles to move both shoulder joints around. First circle forward about fifty times and then reverse the circling motion for another fifty times (Figure 4-85). Keep your mind on your shoulders, and keep them as relaxed as possible. Don't move too fast or you will cause muscle tension, which can hinder the Qi circulation.

You may also circle your shoulders with one of them 180 degrees behind the other (Figure 4-86). This motion has the advantage of moving your chest more, which increases the Qi circulation in the shoulders and helps any stagnant Qi there spread to the chest.

### ii.  Front Waving (Qian Bo)  前波

This exercise comes from crane martial Qigong. Move your arms like a crane's wings when it is flying. It is believed that cranes can fly long distances without rest because they know the key to circulating Qi in the joints where the wings connect to the body. Crane Gongfu emphasizes the shoulders in its Qigong training. This waving exercise is only one of many, but it is a key one in developing the Qi circulation and rebuilding the shoulder joints.

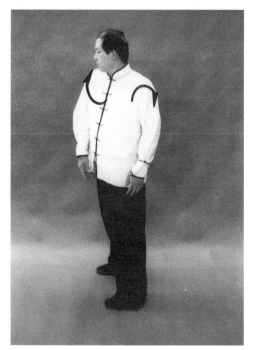

Figure 4-86.

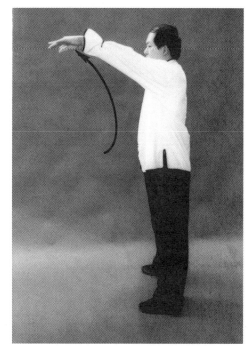

Figure 4-87.

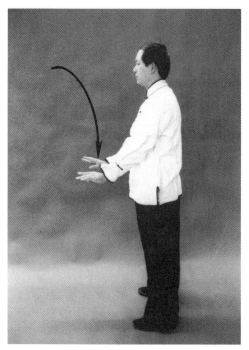

Figure 4-88.

Figure 4-89.

To do front waving, simply extend both arms in front of your chest and wave them up and down like flying wings (Figures 4-87 and 4-88). You may move both arms up and down simultaneously or one up and the other one down (Figure 4-89).

Figure 4-90.                         Figure 4-91.

The key to success is relaxing your shoulder joints as much as possible and moving your arms and chest together. If you can do this, the muscles and tendons in the shoulders will be very relaxed and the Qi circulation will be smooth.

### iii.  Crane Flying (He Xiang)   鶴翔

Crane flying also comes from crane style Qigong. This exercise is similar to the previous one, except now your wings (arms) are to your sides as they are on the bird. You may move both arms up and down at the same time (Figures 4-90 and 4-91), or move one up and the other one down. As in the previous form, treat your arms and chest as one unit and relax the shoulders to their maximum. You should fly until your arms are warm. If you train consistently, after a few months you will be able to increase the number of wing strokes to several hundred without feeling tired. This means that you will have rebuilt your shoulder joints.

### iv.  Front-Back Swinging Arms (Qian Hou Shuai Bi)   前後甩臂

This exercise is adopted from the way your hands swing while you are walking. Simply drop your arms naturally and comfortable beside your body (Figure 4-92), then swing one arm forward while the other swings backward. Turn your body from side to side and let your arms swing naturally. Swing them somewhat higher than you do when walking.

Alternatively, you may swing both arms forward and backward together (Figures 4-93 and 4-94). Arm swinging Qigong has become very popular in Taiwan in the last twenty years since it has been proven to cure many kinds of illnesses, especially those related to

Figure 4-92.                        Figure 4-93.

the lungs and heart. Naturally, this exercise is also used for treating arthritis in the shoulders.

**v.   Front-Side Swing Arms (Qian Ce Shuai Bi)** 前側甩臂

This exercise is very similar to the previous one, however, it comes from martial crane Qigong. In this exercise you swing your arms in an undulating motion to the front and to the sides.

You may swing both arms forward and then sideward at the same time (Figures 4-95 and 4-96) or one forward and the other sideward (Figure 4-97). Extend your fingers but keep them relaxed. Keep your wrists relaxed too, so that they move slightly behind the arms.

After you have rebuilt your shoulder joints you may start to strengthen your muscles and tendons. You can do this by holding a weight in your hands while your are doing the exercises. Start with a light weight and gradually increase it.

**Legs:**

People in China know that walking is one of the most effective exercises for curing arthritis in the shoulders, hips, knees, and ankles. When you walk, your mind is peaceful and your body is relaxed. As you walk, pay attention to your stability, balance, and the motion of your joints. Swing your arms smoothly and lift your legs a little higher than usual. Start walking a mile or so, and increase the distance gradually as you get used to it. When the weather is too cold, or when it is raining, you can walk in place instead. When you feel comfortable walking, you can start walking uphill. On days when you can't go outside, you can walk up and

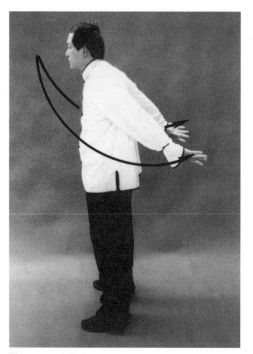

Figure 4-94.

Figure 4-95.

Figure 4-96.

Figure 4-97.

down stairs. In China, when a patient has started walking again, physicians will frequently encourage him or her to walk up a hill in the morning, do some Qigong exercises, and then walk home.

In addition to walking, there are several other Qigong exercises which can be used to cure arthritis in the legs.

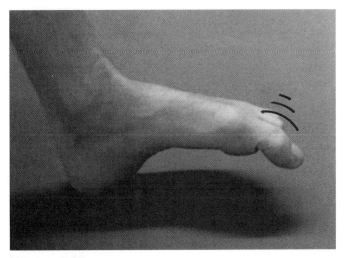

Figure 4-98.

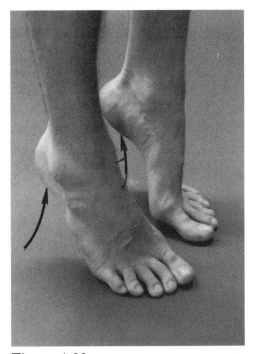

Figure 4-99.

### a. Toes

### i. Squeeze the Toes (Ji Jiao Zhi) 擠腳趾

Bend your toes down toward the centers of your soles and hold them there for about three seconds, and then relax (Figure 4-98). Keep your mind on the joints of the toes, and repeat the exercise until they are warm.

### ii. Up and Down Movements (Ding Zhi) 頂趾

Stand up on your toes for three to five seconds (Figure 4-99) and then lower yourself down onto your feet. This exercise is also very

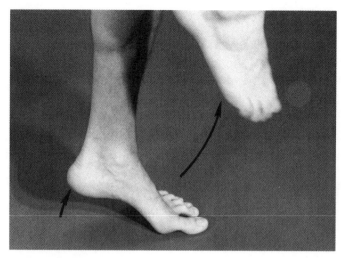

Figure 4-100.

beneficial for arthritis in the ankles. Keep your mind on the joints of your toes, and repeat the exercise until they are warm.

### iii. Walking on the Toes (Zhi Xing) 趾行
This is the simplest exercise for the toes, feet, and ankles. Simply walk on your toes while paying attention to your feet (Figure 4-100). Walk slowly, keeping your body centered and balanced. After you walk about 100 steps, your feet will feel warm. You may then sit down and allow the Qi and blood to circulate upward. After you have rested for a while, you may repeat the exercise.

### b. Ankles
In addition to some of the toe exercises which are also beneficial for the ankles, there is another common Qigong exercise which can be used to improve the Qi and blood circulation in your ankles.

### i. Rotating the Ankles (Zhuan Luo Guan Jie) 轉踝關節
If you are able, stand with your weight on one leg and move the ankle of the other leg in a circle. If you need to, you may use a wall or table for support. Circle in one direction 30 times and then reverse the direction and circle another 30 times (Figure 4-101). If you cannot do this exercise standing, you may do it sitting. Exercise slowly and pay attention to the movement of the joints so that you can feel the Qi moving there.

### c. Knees
### i. Straighten and Bend Movement (Wan Xi) 彎膝
When you do this exercise you may stand on one leg or you may sit on the edge of a chair. Slowly straighten out your leg and then bend it (Figures 4-102 and 4-103). Repeat the exercise until the knee is warm, and then do the same number of repetitions with the other leg. Remember, it is your mind which leads the Qi to the joint, so keep your mind on the exercising joint and feel deeply into it. This way the Qi will be led deep into the joint. Once your knees are

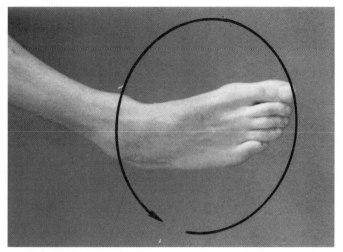

Figure 4-101.

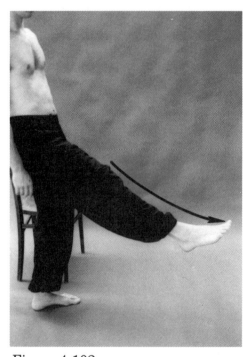

Figure 4-102.

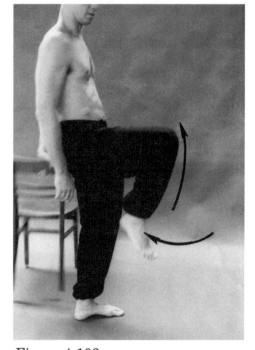

Figure 4-103.

healthy again, you can start strengthening the muscles and tendons by placing a weight on your ankles as you exercise.

**ii. Moving the Body Up and Down (Xia Dun Shang Li)** 下蹲上立
Simply bend your knees and squat down, and then stand up (Figures 4-104 and 4-105). When you start doing this, if your knees are too weak and give you too much pain, only bend them a little. Only when the strength of your knees has been rebuilt should you start squatting lower. Do the exercise slowly and keep your mind on your knees.

Figure 4-104.

Figure 4-105.

Figure 4-106.

### iii. Horse Stance Training (Ma Bu) 馬步

Horse stance training is widely used in the Chinese martial arts to strengthen the knees. To do it, you simply squat down and stay there (Figure 4-106). Arthritis patients whose knees are not very

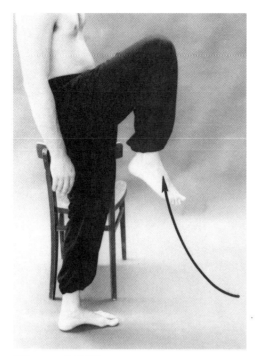

Figure 4-107.                    Figure 4-108.

strong should proceed very cautiously with this exercise. Only squat down slightly, and stay there for only 20 seconds or so. Once the knees are stronger, you can increase the length of time you stand, and also lower your body more to put more pressure on your knees. Horse stance training is one of the most effective techniques for rebuilding the muscles and tendons in the knees.

**d. Hips**

**i. Raise and Lower the Leg (Shang Xia Ti Jiao)** 上下提脚

If possible, stand on one leg, using a wall or table for support if necessary. Simply raise one leg and then lower it (Figures 4-107 and 4-108). Repeat 30 times and then change legs. Keep your mind on your hip joints and do the exercise slowly.

**ii. Sideward Motion and Rotating the Hip (Zuo You Zhuan Tun)** 左右轉臀

Once you are able to lift your leg easily, move it to the side (Figure 4-109) and move it in a circle (Figure 4-110). Move slowly until the joints are strong again, and then increase the speed.

You can see that these Qigong exercises are not very different from the exercises you are already familiar with. What makes them different is that you are not just making a physical motion, you are also using your mind and attention to lead Qi to the joint to repair the damage and strengthen the muscles and tendons. You are also inhaling and exhaling deeply to move the Qi more efficiently into the joints and increase the Qi circulation. It is also important that you move slowly. This keeps the muscles and tendons relaxed, and

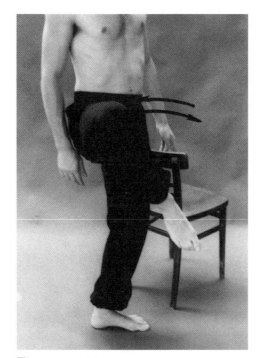 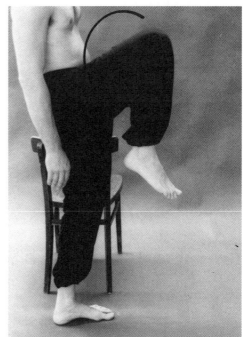

Figure 4-109.                         Figure 4-110.

allows the Qi to move more freely to the joint. When you move slowly it is also easier for you to keep your mind on the joint, and to feel deep inside it. Faster motions are harder to control, and can easily cause more damage.

# Chapter 5
# Conclusion

When you practice Chinese Qigong, understanding the theory and principles is as important as the exercises themselves. If you understand the theory and principles, your mind will not doubt. Only when you feel confident about what you are doing will you continue to practice. Furthermore, if you understand the theory and principles, you can create variations or newer exercises which may suit you better and give you better results. It is not uncommon for people who do not understand the theory and principles to practice Qigong blindly and cause further injury. Therefore, when you practice Qigong, you should study and ponder its theory and principles.

Another thing you should realize is that no one can understand you, especially mentally, better than you can. The best way to heal yourself is to know yourself and understand the key to your individual problem. Then you can adapt the recommended methods to fit your particular problem and your personality. If you can do this, then the Qigong exercises which can benefit you will be naturally carried over into your lifestyle and become part of your life. This is the only way that you will continue to practice, and the only way that the benefits will really last.

As I mentioned in the beginning of this book, Chinese medicine has many ways or treating arthritis, and I know only a few of them. I hope that people who are qualified in other fields such as acupuncture and herbal treatment will contribute their knowledge and experience to fill this void.

In addition to introducing the West to the Qigong exercises for healing arthritis, I have had another goal in writing this book. I sincerely hope that this book will gain the attention of the Western medical establishment, and encourage them to get involved in Qigong experimentation, study, and research. This book is not an authority on this subject. It is, however, an attempt to open communication between East and West on the subject of medicine and healing. I deeply believe that if all of the different cultures can share their knowledge and experience and cooperate with each other, medical science will take a great step forward for the benefit of all humankind.

# Appendix A
# Glossary of Chinese Terms

In order to be consistent with international usage, we have decided that in this book we will begin to use the Pinyin system for spelling Chinese words. We hope that this will be more convenient for those readers who consult other Chinese books. The spellings used in previously published YMAA books will be given in parentheses. However, in order to avoid further confusion, commonly recognized spellings of names will not be changed, such as Tamkang College and Taipei. In addition, the spelling which individuals have chosen for their names will not be changed either, such as my name Yang Jwing-Ming, Wen-Ching Wu, etc.

**An Mo (Ann Mo):** 按摩

Literally: press rub. Together they mean massage.

**Ba Duan Jin (Ba Duann Gin):** 八段錦

Eight Pieces of Brocade. A Wai Dan Qigong practice which is said to have been created by Marshal Yeuh Fei during the Song dynasty (1127-1279 A.D.).

**Ba Gua (Ba Kua):** 八卦

Literally: Eight Divinations. Also called the Eight Trigrams. In Chinese philosophy, the eight basic variations; shown in the Yi Jing as groups of single and broken lines.

**Ba Gua Zhang (Ba Kua Chang):** 八卦掌

Eight Trigrams Palm. One of the internal Qigong martial styles, believed to have been created by Dong Hai-Chuan between 1866 and 1880 A.D.

**Bai He (Pai Huo):** 白鶴

White Crane. A style of southern Shaolin Gongfu which imitates the fighting techniques of the crane.

**Chan (Charn)(Zen):** 禪（忍）

A Chinese school of Mahayana Buddhism which asserts that enlightenment can be attained through meditation, self-contemplation, and intuition, rather than through study of scripture. Chan is called Zen in Japan.

**Chang Quan (Chang Chuan):** 長拳

Chang means long, and Quan means fist, style, or sequence. A style of Northern Chinese Gongfu which specializes in kicking and long range fighting. Chang Quan has also been used to refer to Taijiquan.

**Chang San-Feng:** 張三豐

Said to have created Taijiquan in the Song dynasty (960-1279 A.D.), however there is no certain documentary proof of this.

**Da Mo:** 達摩

The Indian Buddhist monk who is credited with creating the Yi Jin Jing and Xi Sui Jing while at the Shaolin monastery. His last name was Sardili, and he was also known as Bodhidarma. He was formerly the prince of a small tribe in southern India.

**Dan Ding Dao Gong (Dan Diing Tao Kung):** 丹鼎道功

The elixir cauldron way of Qigong. The Daoists' Qigong training.

**Dan Tian (Dan Tien):** 丹田

Literally: Field of Elixir. Locations in the body which are able to store and generate Qi (elixir) in the body. The Upper, Middle, and Lower Dan Tians are located respectively between the eyebrows, at the solar plexus, and a few inches below the navel.

**Dao (Tao):** 道

The way. The "natural" way of everything.

**Dao De Jing (Tao Te Ching):** 道德經

Morality Classic. Written by Lao Zi.

**Dao Jia or Dao Jiao (Tao Jia or Tao Jiaw):** 道家（道教）

The Dao family. Daoism. Created by Lao Zi during the Zhou dynasty (1122-934 B.C.). In the Han dynasty (c. 58 A.D.), it was mixed with Buddhism to become the Daoist religion (Dao Jiao).

**Di (Dih):** 地

The Earth. Earth, Heaven (Tian), and Man (Ren) are the "Three Natural Powers" (San Cai).

**Di Li Shi (Dih Lii Shy):** 地理師

Di Li means geomancy and Shi means teacher. Therefore Di Li Shi means a teacher or master who analyzes geographic locations according to formulas in the Yi Jing (Book of Change) and the energy distributions in the Earth.

**Di Qi (Dih Chi):** 地氣

Earth Qi. The energy of the earth.

**Dian Mai (Dim Mak):** 點脉

Pointing the Vessels. The way of striking Qi or blood vessels in Chinese martial arts. See also Dian Xue.

**Dian Xue (Dien Shiuh):** 點穴

Dian means "to point and exert pressure" and Xue means "the cavities." Dian Xue refers to those Qin Na techniques which specialize in attacking acupuncture cavities to immobilize or kill an opponent.

**E Mei Shan (Ermei Mountain):** 峨嵋山

A mountain located in Szechuan province in China. Many

martial Qigong styles originated there.

**Fan Jing Bu Nao (Faan Jieng Buu Nao):** 返精補腦

Literally: to return the Essence to nourish the brain. A Daoist Qigong training process wherein Qi which has been converted from Essence is led to the head to nourish the brain.

**Feng Shi:** 風濕

Literally: wind moisture. In Chinese medicine, the stage before arthritis (called "Guan Jie Yan") where there is no symptom of physical damage, although a Qi disturbance has been felt or diagnosed.

**Feng Shui Shi (Feng Shoei Shy):** 風水師

Literally: wind water teacher. Teacher or master of geomancy. Geomancy is the art or science of analyzing the natural energy relationships in a location, especially the interrelationships between "wind" and "water," hence the name. Also called Di Li Shi.

**Gongfu (Kung Fu):** 功夫

Literally: energy-time. Any study, learning, or practice which requires a lot of patience, energy, and time to complete. Since practicing Chinese martial arts requires a great deal of time and energy, Chinese martial arts are commonly called Gongfu.

**Guan Jie Yan:** 關節炎

Joint infection. Chinese name for arthritis.

**Gui Qi (Goe Chi):** 鬼氣

The Qi residue of a dead person. It is believed by the Chinese Buddhists and Daoists that this Qi residue is a so called ghost.

**Guoshu (Kuoshu):** 國術

Literally: national techniques. Another name for Chinese martial arts. First used by President Chiang Kai-Shek in 1926 at the founding of the Nanking Central Kuoshu Institute.

**Huang Ting (Hwang Tyng):** 黃庭

Yellow yard. 1. A yard or hall in which Daoists, who often wore yellow robes, meditate together. 2. In Qigong training, a spot in the abdomen where it is believed that you are able to generate an "embryo."

**Jia Gu Wen (Jea Guu Wen):** 甲骨文

Oracle-Bone Scripture. Earliest evidence of the Chinese use of the written word. Found on pieces of turtle shell and animal bone from the Shang dynasty (1766-1154 B.C.). Most of the information recorded was of a religious nature.

**Jin Zhong Zhao (Gin Jong Jaw):** 金鐘罩

Golden Bell Cover. An Iron Shirt training.

**Jing:** 勁

A power in Chinese martial arts which is derived from muscles which have been energized by Qi to their maximum potential.

**Jing (Ching):** 經

Channel. Sometimes translated meridian. Refers to the twelve organ-related "rivers" which circulate Qi throughout the body.

**Jing (Jieng):** 精

Essence. The most refined part of anything.

**Jing Zi (Jieng Tzu):** 精子

Sons of the essence. Refers to the sperm.

**Lao Zi (Lao Tzyy):** 老子

The creator of Daoism, also called Li Er.

**Li Er (Li Erh):** 李耳

Lao Zi, the creator of Daoism.

**Lian Qi (Liann Chi):** 練氣

Liann means to train, to strengthen, and to refine. A Daoist training process through which your Qi grows stronger and more abundant.

**Liu He Ba Fa (Liu Ho Ba Fa):** 六合八法

Literally: six combinations eight methods. A style of Chinese internal martial arts reportedly created by Chen Bo during the Song dynasty (960-1279 A.D.).

**Luo (Lou):** 絡

The small Qi channels which branch out from the primary Qi channels and are connected to the skin and to the bone marrow.

**Mai (Mei):** 脉

Qi vessels. The eight vessels involved with transporting, storing, and regulating Qi.

**Mi Zong Shen Gong (Mih Tzong Shen Kung):** 密宗神功

Secret Style of Spiritual Gongfu. Tibetan Qigong and martial arts.

**Nei Dan:** 內丹

Internal elixir. A form of Qigong in which Qi (the elixir) is built up in the body and spread out to the limbs.

**Nei Gong (Nei Kung):** 內功

Internal Gongfu. The Chinese martial styles which emphasize building up Qi internally in the beginning, and later use this Qi to energize the muscles to a higher degree of efficiency. See also Wai Gong.

**Nei Shi Gongfu (Nei Shyh Kung Fu):** 內視功夫

Nei Shyh means to look internally, so Nei Shi Gongfu refers to the art of looking inside yourself to read the state of your health and the condition of your Qi.

**Qi (Chi):** 氣

The general definition of Qi is: universal energy, including heat, light, and electromagnetic energy. A narrower definition of Qi refers to the energy circulating in human or animal bodies.

**Qigong (Chi Kung):** 氣功

Gong means Gongfu (lit. energy-time). Therefore, Qigong means study, research, and/or practices related to Qi.

**Qi Huo (Chii Huoo):** 起火

To start the fire. In Qigong practice: when you start to build up Qi at the Lower Dan Tian.

**Qin Na (Chin Na):** 擒拿

Literally, grab control. A type of Chinese Gongfu which emphasizes grabbing techniques to control the opponent's joints in conjunction with attacking certain acupuncture cavities.

**Ren Mai (Ren Mei):** 任脉

Usually translated "Conception Vessel."

**Ren Qi (Ren Chi):** 人氣

Human Qi.

**Ru Jia:** 儒家

Literally: Confucian family. Scholars following the ideas of Confucian thoughts; Confucianists.

**San Bao:** 三寶

Three treasures. Essence (Jing), energy (Qi), and spirit (Shen). Also called San Yuan (three origins).

**San Cai (San Tsair):** 三才

Three powers. Heaven, Earth, and Man.

**San Gong (Sann Kung):** 散功

Energy dispersion. Premature degeneration of the muscles when the Qi cannot effectively energize them. Caused by earlier overtraining.

**Shaolin:** 少林

A Buddhist temple in Henan province, famous for its martial arts.

**Shen:** 神

Spirit. Said to reside in the Upper Dan Tian (the third eye).

**Shen Xin Ping Heng (Shenn Hsin Pyng Herng):** 身心平衡

The body and the mind are mutually balanced. In Chinese Qigong, the physical body is Yang and the mind is Yin. They must both be trained to balance each other.

**Shen Xi Xiang Yi (Shen Shyi Shiang Yi):** 神息相依

The Shen and breathing mutually rely on each other. A stage in Qigong practice.

**Suan Ming Shi (Suann Ming Shy):** 算命師

Literally: calculate life teacher. A fortune teller who is able to calculate your future and destiny.

**Taijiquan (Tai Chi Chuan):** 太极拳

Great ultimate fist. An internal martial art.

**Tian Qi (Tian Chi):** 天氣

Heaven Qi. It is now commonly used to mean the weather, since weather is governed by heaven Qi.

**Tian Shi (Tian Shyr):** 天時

Heavenly timing. The repeated natural cycles generated by the heavens such as the seasons, months, days, and hours.

**Tie Bu Shan (Tiea Bu Shan):** 鐵布衫

Iron shirt. Gongfu training which toughens the body externally and internally.

**Tui Na (Tuei Na):** 推拿

Literally: push and grab. A style of massage and manipulation for treatment of injuries and many illnesses.

**Tiao Qi (Tyau Chi):** 調氣

To regulate the Qi.

**Tiao Shen (Tyau Shen):** 調神

To regulate the spirit.

**Tiao Shen (Tyau Shen):** 調身

To regulate the body.

**Tiao Xi (Tyau Shyi):** 調息

To regulate the breathing.

**Tiao Xin (Tyau Hsin):** 調心

　　To regulate the emotional mind.

**Wai Dan:** 外丹

　　External elixir. External Qigong exercises in which Qi is built up in the limbs and then led to the body.

**Wai Gong (Wai Kung):** 外功

　　External Gongfu. The Chinese martial styles which emphasize mainly muscular power and strength in the beginning. See also Nei Gong.

**Wei Qi (Wey Chi):** 衛氣

　　Guardian Qi. The Qi shield which wards off negative external influences.

**Wudang (Wuudang Mountain):** 武當

　　Located in Fubei province in China.

**Wushu:** 武術

　　Literally: martial techniques. A common name for the Chinese martial arts. Many other terms are used, including: Wuyi (martial arts), Wugong (martial Gongfu), Guoshu (national techniques), and Gongfu (energy-time). Because Wushu has been modified in mainland China over the past forty years into gymnastic martial performance, many traditional Chinese martial artist have given up this name in order to avoid confusing modern Wushu with traditional Wushu. Recently, mainland China has attempted to bring modern Wushu back toward its traditional training and practice.

**Xi Sui Jing (Shii Soei Ching):** 洗髓經

　　Washing Marrow/Brain Classic, usually translated Marrow/Brain Washing Classic. Qigong training specializing in leading Qi to the marrow to cleanse it.

**Xian Tian Qi (Shian Tian Chi):** 先天氣

　　Pre-birth Qi. Also called Dan Tian Qi. The Qi which was converted from Original Essence and is stored in the Lower Dan Tian. Considered to be "Water Qi," it is able to calm the body.

**Xin (Hsin):** 心

　　Literally: Heart. Refers to the emotional mind.

**Xin Xi Xiang Yi (Hsin Shyi Shiang Yi):** 心息相依

　　The emotional mind and breathing mutually relying on each other. A method of regulating the mind in Qigong in which the practitioner pays attention to his breathing in order to clear his mind of disturbance.

**Xing Yi or Xing Yi Quan (Hsing Yi or Hsing Yi Chuan):** 形意（形意拳）

　　Literally: Shape-Mind Fist. An internal style of Gongfu in which the mind or thinking determines the shape or movement of the body. Creation of the style attributed to Marshal Yeuh Fei.

**Xiu Qi (Shiou Chi):** 修氣

　　Cultivate the Qi. Cultivate implies to protect, maintain, and refine. A Buddhist Qigong training.

**Yang:** 陽

　　In Chinese philosophy, the active, positive, masculine polarity.

In Chinese medicine, Yang means excessive, overactive, overheated. The Yang (or outer) organs are the Gall Bladder, Small Intestine, Large Intestine, Stomach, Bladder, and Triple Burner.

**Yi: 意**

Mind. Specifically, the mind which is generated by clear thinking and judgement, and which is able to make you calm, peaceful, and wise.

**Yi Jin Jing (Yi Gin Ching): 易筋經**

Literally: changing muscle/tendon classic, usually called The Muscle/Tendon Changing Classic. Credited to Da Mo around 550 A.D., this work discusses Wai Dan Qigong training for strengthening the physical body.

**Yi Jing (I Ching): 易經**

Book of Changes. A book of divination written during the Zhou dynasty (1122-255 B.C.).

**Yi Shou Dan Tian (Yi Shoou Dan Tien): 意守丹田**

Keep your Yi on your Dan Tian. In Qigong training, you keep your mind at the Dan Tian in order to build up Qi. When you are circulating your Qi, you always lead your Qi back to your Dan Tian before you stop.

**Yi Yi Yin Qi (Yii Yi Yiin Chi): 以意引氣**

Use your Yi (wisdom mind) to lead your Qi. A Qigong technique. Qi cannot be pushed, but it can be led. This is best done with the Yi.

**Yin: 陰**

In Chinese philosophy, the passive, negative, feminine polarity. In Chinese medicine, Yin means deficient. The Yin (internal) organs are the Heart, Lungs, Liver, Kidneys, Spleen, and Pericardium.

**Ying Gong (Ying Kung): 硬功**

Hard Gongfu. The Chinese martial styles which emphasize hard Jing training.

**Ying Qi (Ying Chi): 營氣**

Managing Qi. It manages the functioning of the organs and the body.

**Yuan Jing (Yuan Jieng): 元精**

Original Essence. The fundamental, original substance inherited from your parents, it is converted into Original Qi.

**Yuan Qi (Yuan Chi): 元氣**

Original Qi. The Qi created from the Original Essence inherited from your parents.

**Yue Fei (Yeuh Fei): 岳飛**

A Chinese hero in the Southern Song dynasty (1127-1279 A.D.). Said to have created Ba Duan Jin, Xing Yi Quan, and Yue's Ying Zhua.

# Appendix B
# Translation of Chinese Terms

| | |
|---|---|
| 楊俊敏 | Yang Jwing-Ming |
| 太极拳 | Taijiquan (Tai Chi Chuan) |
| 内劲 | Nei Jing |
| 吳文慶 | Wen-Ching Wu |
| 功夫 | Gongfu (Kung Fu) |
| 武術 | Wushu |
| 少林 | Shaolin |
| 白鶴 | Bai He (Pai Huo) |
| 曾金灶 | Cheng Gin-Gsao |
| 高濤 | Kao Tao |
| 小週天 | Xiao Zhou Tian (Sheau Jou Tian) |
| 淡江學院 | Tamkang College |
| 臺北縣 | Taipei Hsien |
| 長拳 | Chang Quan (Chang Chuan) |
| 李茂清 | Li Mao-Ching |
| 陳威伸 | Wilson Chen |
| 張祥三 | Zhang Xiang-San (Chang Shyang-Shan) |
| 易筋經 | Yi Jin Jing (Yi Gin Ching) |
| 洗髓經 | Xi Sui Jing (Shii Soei Ching) |
| 推拿 | Tui Na (Tuei Na) |
| 按摩 | An Mo (Ann Mo) |
| 點穴 | Dian Xue (Dien Shiuh) |
| 武當 | Wudang (Wuudang) |
| 峨嵋 | E Mei (Ermei) |
| 禪 | Chan (Charn) |
| 丹鼎道功 | Dan Ding Dao Gong (Dan Diing Tao Kung) |
| 密宗神功 | Mi Zong Shen Gong (Mih Tzong |

| | |
|---|---|
| 五禽戲 | Wu Qin Xi (Wuu Chyn Shih) |
| 葛洪 | Ge Hong (Ger Horng) |
| 抱朴子 | Bao Pu Zi (Baw Poh Tzyy) |
| 陶弘景 | Tao Hong-Jing (Taur Horng-Jiing) |
| 養身延命錄 | Yang Shen Yan Ming Lu (Yeang Shenn Yan Ming Luh) |
| 達摩 | Da Mo |
| 隋 | Sui (Swei) |
| 唐 | Tang (Tarng) |
| 巢元方 | Chao Yuan-Fang (Chaur Yuan-Fang) |
| 諸病源候論 | Zhu Bing Yuan Hou Lun (Ju Bing Yuan Hou Luenn) |
| 千金方 | Qian Jin Fang (Chian Gin Fang) |
| 孫思邈 | Sun Si-Mao (Suen Sy-Meau) |
| 外臺密要 | Wai Tai Mi Yao (Wai Tai Mih Yao) |
| 王燾 | Wang Tao (Wang Taur) |
| 宋 | Song |
| 金 | Jin (Gin) |
| 元 | Yuan |
| 養身訣 | Yang Shen Jue (Yeang Shenn Jyue) |
| 張安道 | Zhang An-Dao (Chang An-Tao) |
| 儒門視事 | Ru Men Shi Shi (Ru Men Shyh Shyh) |
| 張子和 | Zhang Zi-He (Chang Tzyy-Her) |
| 蘭室密藏 | Lan Shi Mi Cang (Lan Shyh Mih Tsarng) |
| 李果 | Li Guo (Li Guoo) |
| 格致餘論 | Ge Zhi Yu Lun (Ger Jyh Yu Luenn) |
| 朱丹溪 | Zhu Dan-Xi (Ju Dan-Shi) |
| 張三豐 | Chang San-Feng |
| 外丹 | Wai Dan |
| 內丹 | Nei Dan |
| 王唯一 | Wang Wei-Yi |
| 銅人俞穴針灸圖 | Tong Ren Yu Xue Zhen Jiu Tu (Torng Ren Yu Shiuh Jen Jeou Twu) |
| 仁宗 | Ren Zong (Ren Tzong) |
| 南宋 | Nan Song (Southern Song) |
| 岳飛 | Yue Fei (Yeuh Fei) |
| 虎步功 | Hu Bu Gong (Hwu Buh Kung) |
| 十二压 | Shi Er Zhuang (Shyr Er Juang) |
| 叫化功 | Jiao Hua Gong (Jiaw Huah Kung) |
| 保身秘要 | Bao Shen Mi Yao (Bao Shenn Mih Yao) |
| 曹元白 | Cao Yuan-Bai (Tsaur Yuan-Bair) |
| 養身膚語 | Yang Shen Fu Yu (Yeang Shenn Fu Yeu) |
| 陳繼儒 | Chen Ji-Ru (Chen Jih-Ru) |
| 醫方集介 | Yi Fan Ji Jie (Yi Fang Jyi Jieh) |

| | |
|---|---|
| 汪汎庵 | Wang Fan-An (Uang Fann-An) |
| 內功圖說 | Nei Gong Tu Shuo (Nei Kung Twu Shwo) |
| 王祖源 | Wang Zu-Yuan (Wang Tzuu-Yuan) |
| 明 | Ming |
| 火龍功 | Huo Long Gong (Huoo Long Kung) |
| 太陽 | Taiyang |
| 八卦掌 | Ba Gua Zhang (Ba Kua Chang) |
| 董海川 | Dong Hai-Chuan (Doong Hae-Chuan) |
| 孔子 | Confucians |
| 孟子 | Mencius |
| 儒家 | Ru Jia |
| 道家 | Dao Jia (Tao Jia) |
| 修氣 | Xiu Qi (Shiou Chi) |
| 練氣 | Lian Qi (Liann Chi) |
| 安天樂命 | An Tian Le Ming (An Tian Leh Ming) |
| 修身俟命 | Xiu Shen Shi Ming (Shiou Shenn Shy Ming) |
| 八段錦 | Ba Duan Jin (Ba Duann Gin) |
| 葉明 | Ye Ming (Yeh Ming) |
| 點脈 | Dian Mai (Dim Mak) |
| 鐵布衫 | Tie Bu Shan (Tiea Bu Shan) |
| 金鐘罩 | Jin Zhong Zhao (Gin Jong Jaw) |
| 外功 | Wai Gong (Wai Kung) |
| 硬功 | Ying Gong (Ying Kung) |
| 散功 | San Gong (Sann Kung) |
| 營氣 | Ying Qi (Ying Chi) |
| 衛氣 | Wei Qi (Wey Chi) |
| 調身 | Tiao Shen (Tyau Shenn) |
| 調心 | Tiao Xin (Tyau Hsin) |
| 調息 | Tiao Xi (Tyau Shyi) |
| 調氣 | Tiao Qi (Tyau Chi) |
| 調神 | Tiao Shen (Tyau Shen) |
| 三寶 | San Bao |
| 三元 | San Yuan |
| 精子 | Jing Zi (Jieng Tzyy) |
| 元精 | Yuan Jing (Yuan Jieng) |
| 元氣 | Yuan Qi (Yuan Chi) |
| 先天氣 | Xian Tian Qi (Shian Tian Chi) |
| 返精補腦 | Fan Jing Bu Nao (Faan Jieng Buu Nao) |
| 丹田 | Dan Tian (Dan Tien) |
| 鬼氣 | Gui Qi (Goe Chi) |
| 身心平衡 | Shen Xin Ping Heng (Shenn Hsin Pyng Herng) |
| 心息相依 | Xin Xi Xiang Yi (Hsin Shyi Shiang Yi) |
| 李清庵 | Li Qing-An (Li Ching-Yen) |

| | |
|---|---|
| 天旋地轉 | Tian Xuan Di Zhuan |
| 大龍軟身 | Da Long Ruan Shen |
| 大龍轉身 | Da Long Zhuan Shen |
| 扭腰現活 | Niu Yao Xian Huo |
| 獅子搖頭 | Shi Zi Yao Tou |
| 前躬後鞠 | Qian Gong Hou Ju |
| 章魚游水 | Zhang Yu You Shui |
| 指波翔功 | Zhi Bo Xiang Gong |
| 虎爪行功 | Hu Zhua Xing Gong |
| 轉太极球 | Zhuan Taiji Qiu |
| 轉腕 | Zhuan Wan |
| 交指轉腕 | Jiao Zhi Zhuan Wan |
| 交手轉腕 | Jiao Shou Zhuan Wan |
| 上提彎肘 | Shang Ti Wan Zhou |
| 內外彎肘 | Nei Wai Wan Zhou |
| 轉肘 | Zhuan Zhou |
| 聳肩 | Song Jian |
| 前波 | Qian Bo |
| 鶴翔 | He Xiang |
| 前後甩臂 | Qian Hou Shuai Bi |
| 前側甩臂 | Qian Ce Shuai Bi |
| 擠脚趾 | Ji Jiao Zhi |
| 頂趾 | Ding Zhi |
| 趾行 | Zhi Xing |
| 轉踝關節 | Zhuan Luo Guan Jie |
| 彎膝 | Wan Xi |
| 下蹲上立 | Xia Dun Shang Li |
| 馬步 | Ma Bu |
| 上下提脚 | Shang Xia Ti Jiao |
| 左右轉臀 | Zuo You Zhuan Tun |

**Appendix A**

| | |
|---|---|
| 四川 | Szechuan |
| 蔣介石 | Chiang Kai-Shek |
| 南京中央國術館 | Nanking Central Kuoshu Inst. |
| 陳博 | Chen Bo (Chen Bor) |
| 武藝 | Wuyi |
| 武功 | Wugong (Wukung) |
| 湖北 | Fubei |
| 岳家鷹爪 | Yue's Ying Zhua (Yeuh's Ien Jao) |

# Index

# *Other Titles Available from YMAA*

## Unique Publications

**B001.** *SHAOLIN CHIN NA*
**B002.** *SHAOLIN LONG FIST KUNG FU*
**B003.** *YANG STYLE TAI CHI CHUAN*
**B004.** *INTRODUCTION TO ANCIENT CHINESE WEAPONS*

## YMAA Publication Center Book Series

**B005.** *CHI KUNG — Health and Martial Arts*
**B006.** *NORTHERN SHAOLIN SWORD*
**B007.** *ADVANCED YANG STYLE TAI CHI CHUAN — Tai Chi Theory and Tai Chi Jing, Volume 1*
**B008.** *ADVANCED YANG STYLE TAI CHI CHUAN — Martial Applications, Volume 2*
**B009.** *ANALYSIS OF SHAOLIN CHIN NA — Instructor's Manual*
**B010.** *THE EIGHT PIECES OF BROCADE*
**B011.** *THE ROOT OF CHINESE CHI KUNG — The Secrets of Chi Kung Training*
**B012.** *MUSCLE/TENDON CHANGING AND MARROW/BRAIN WASHING CHI KUNG — The Secret of Youth*
**B013.** *HSING YI CHUAN — Theory and Applications*
**B014.** *THE ESSENCE OF TAI CHI CHI KUNG — Health and Martial Arts*
**B015.** *QIGONG FOR ARTHRITIS — The Chinese Way of Healing and Prevention*
**B016.** *CHINESE QIGONG MASSAGE — General Massage*
**B017.** *HOW TO DEFEND YOURSELF — Effective & Practical Martial Arts Strategies*
**B018.** *THE TAO OF BIOENERGETICS — East – West*
**B019.** *A GUIDE TO TAIJIQUAN — 24 & 48 Posture with Applications*
**B020.** *BAGUAZHANG — Emei Baguazhang*
**B021.** *COMPREHENSIVE APPLICATIONS OF SHAOLIN CHIN NA — The Practical Defense of Chinese Seizing Arts for All Styles*
**B022.** *TAIJI CHIN NA — The Seizing Art of Taijiquan*
**B023.** *PROFESSIONAL BUDO — Ethics, Chivalry, and the Samurai Code*
**B024.** *SONG OF A WATER DRAGON*

## YMAA Publication Center Children's Book Series

**CB001.** *CARVING THE BUDDHA*
**CB002.** *THE MASK OF THE KING*
**CB003.** *THE FOX BORROWS THE TIGER'S AWE*

## YMAA Publication Center Videotape Series

**T001.** *YANG STYLE TAI CHI CHUAN — and Its Applications*
**T002.** *SHAOLIN LONG FIST KUNG FU — Lien Bu Chuan and Its Applications*
**T003.** *SHAOLIN LONG FIST KUNG FU — Gung Li Chuan and Its Applications*
**T004.** *SHAOLIN CHIN NA*
**T005.** *THE EIGHT PIECES OF BROCADE*
**T006.** *CHI KUNG FOR TAI CHI CHUAN*
**T007.** *QIGONG FOR ARTHRITIS — The Chinese Way of Healing and Prevention*
**T008.** *CHINESE QIGONG MASSAGE — Self Massage*
**T009.** *CHINESE QIGONG MASSAGE — Massage with a Partner*
**T010.** *HOW TO DEFEND YOURSELF 1 — Unarmed Attack*
**T011.** *HOW TO DEFEND YOURSELF 2 — Knife Attack*
**T012.** *COMPREHENSIVE APPLICATIONS OF SHAOLIN CHIN NA 1*
**T013.** *COMPREHENSIVE APPLICATIONS OF SHAOLIN CHIN NA 2*
**T014.** *SHAOLIN LONG FIST KUNG FU — Er Lu Mai Fu*
**T015.** *SHAOLIN LONG FIST KUNG FU — Shi Zi Tang*
**T016.** *TAIJI CHIN NA*
**T017.** *EMEI BAGUAZHANG 1*
**T018.** *EMEI BAGUAZHANG 2*
**T019.** *EMEI BAGUAZHANG 3*
**T020.** *XINGYI 12 ANIMAL FORM*
**T021.** *TAIJIQUAN — 24 & 48 Forms*